PURE GOLF

PURE GOLF

by JOHNNY MILLER
with Dale Shankland

Foreword by John Geertsen

Illustrations by Jim McQueen

HODDER AND STOUGHTON
LONDON SYDNEY AUCKLAND TORONTO

DEDICATED TO

My father, my pro John, and my coach
Karl, whose confidence and support
make the difference

Designed by Joseph P. Ascherl

Foreword

I first met Johnny Miller and his parents at the Mormon Church in San Francisco. One month earlier the Millers had suffered the loss of their eldest son, who had drowned in a fishing accident. At this time, I was the golf professional at San Francisco Golf Club. Larry Miller was looking for a way to get young Johnny, who was at this time age seven, over the deep emotional loss and asked about the possibilities of golf lessons. I was told the boy had been hitting balls into a net in the basement of their home for approximately two years and had been schooled in the basic fundamentals of the golf swing.

It should be noted that Johnny, at age seven, was a skinny boy, and frankly I was quite skeptical about how much I could do to help him. In addition, from past experience I knew that children at that age are more interested in watching an airplane fly overhead than in seeing if their hands are correctly positioned on a golf club. But when Johnny and his dad came out to San Francisco Golf Club the following week, I quickly discovered that this boy was different.

Johnny watched and listened intently to everything I said. It was easy to see that he was anxious to learn and that he implicitly trusted my ability as a teacher. From this point forth, we enjoyed a tremendous teacher/student relationship.

Johnny's desire to understand the essentials of the golf swing and his ability to retain the important points from every lesson enabled him to create by age ten almost the same swing that you see him use on the tour today.

As a teacher, you see a lot of juniors who have the makings of champions. Many, however, reach their peaks in their middle teens but never improve beyond that. One reason for this is that the goals they set for themselves are unrealistic. In this respect, Johnny was always unique. He was constantly analyzing and re-evaluating his goals. Thus, the disappointments that he suffered were a lot less disturbing than for the player who set his sights higher than his playing ability would allow.

His attitude is also one reason why he scores so many low rounds. Today, he's graduated to a level where he is no longer intimidated by his own ability. When he's good he knows that he must become very good, then excellent, and then "superexcellent." I wouldn't be a bit surprised if at some point in competition he scores in the fifties!

On the physical side, Johnny worked extremely hard to train the proper muscles for golf. As a result, as he has grown stronger, so has his game. Today, he has possibly the most phenomenal swing in golf. Yet he is far from his peak.

Johnny has always been a great student of the game and does everything he can to increase his knowledge of the golf swing. He devours golf magazines and instruction books in much the same way as an avid fan reads the sports pages.

We are all fortunate to be able to take advantage of Johnny's wealth of knowledge. And there is no doubt that he has prepared this manuscript in much the same way that he did to become the true champion that he is—with dedication. The golfing world can only benefit from his advice and knowledge. He's a model golfer and a model human being with a character and way of life that are beyond reproach.

JOHN GEERTSEN

Acknowledgments

The author would like to acknowledge the assistance of the following people, whose contributions to this book are invaluable:

Dale Shankland, an English-born golf professional, writer, and former staff instructional editor for *Golf* magazine, who spent many months interviewing me and studying my game to transmit my theories through the written word.

Jim McQueen, also a golf professional as well as an illustrator, who has captured my theories so distinctively with brush.

Desmond Tolhurst, senior editor of *Golf* magazine, who rendered invaluable technical assistance while the manuscript was being written.

Dr. Richard Agnew, who made many trips to tournament sites to gather important art reference.

John Geertsen, my teacher and long-time friend, who provided the essentials of my early playing years for analysis.

Finally, the author would like to thank the members of both San Francisco Golf Club and the Olympic Club for their help and support over the years.

Contents

CHAPTER ONE

A Step-by-Step Course to Consistency

When I look back on my own career in golf, I can't think of anything I'd change in the opportunities I've had. I mean I was just given every single possible opportunity to succeed. For that reason, I want to tell you, within the limits of this book, everything I can to ensure that you learn the right principles and really grow as a golfer. If you build your golfing house on a sound foundation, you will always derive pleasure from the game. If you don't, your progression will be limited.

There are two ways, really, that you can gain knowledge. The first is to go to a good teaching professional. In my own case my father, having taught me the fundamentals in the basement of our house for two years, took me to see John Geertsen, who was the professional at San Francisco Golf Club. To this day John is still my teacher. He knows my swing better than anybody else. The second way is from books. Here too, my father saw to it that I had the opportunity to take advantage of the great players' knowledge by exposing me to the best books during my early years.

In developing your swing it's also perfectly natural for you to emulate the best golfers, as I did, both in person and through such media as books, magazines, TV, etc. Not only is this natural, it's a great way to learn.

I know that, in my own case, this process of emulating the great players was vital in my development. When I was really small, from around six to twelve years old, I always thought Cary Middlecoff looked pretty neat. I didn't know much about the swing at the time, but I remember reading a magazine article about Cary which said "Middlecoff splits the pin." At that time I figured that anybody who could split the pin, like Robin Hood split the arrow, had to be pretty good. Cary had that big knee action and threw his hips way out in front of him as he hit the ball. That's where I got that big lateral move into the downswing with my knees.

My first golf lesson was when I was seven and a half years old, and at that time Tony Lema was the assistant pro at San Francisco Golf Club. Later, when I was about fifteen or sixteen, I played golf with him a couple of times and tried to copy his swing—that outside to inside, figure-eight type move. I've always been open-minded.

When I got older, I got very interested in Sam Snead, Ben Hogan, and Jimmie Demaret, the fine swings. Besides studying their swings in books and magazines, my father took me to see the top pros in person whenever there was an opportunity. One point I would like to hammer home—you've got to learn from the best people. If you can't learn from the best, then whom can you learn from? Be critical in your study, though. Nobody is going to be the best at everything. One player, for example, may have a great swing but may not be a good putter. Another could have the greatest short game in the world yet not be a good striker of the ball when using a full swing.

It's important to realize that in emulating the great players you should not try and carbon-copy the great players' swings or technique in the various parts of the game. What you do is study what each player does supremely well, and apply the principles of what you learn to your own game. In most cases, you will adapt these to some extent. After all, no two people will have identical physiques or temperaments.

You use the principles you've discovered to improve the weak parts of your swing or a particular aspect of your game. And here I would like to digress for a moment to point out that it's essential for you to know, at any time, the true state of your game. You do this by continuous analysis of your rounds. As you play each hole, note the clubs you hit, number of chips, sand shots, etc., you had, the length of your first putt, and the total number of putts you took. In this way you can look back on your round and see what needs improving. For example, if you have a lot of chip shots, you're missing a lot of greens and probably your irons need work. If you see a lot of chips followed by two putts, then your chipping is weak, and so on.

Getting back to the swing, I think it's important for any aspiring golfer to realize that today's longer courses have made golf much more of a power game than in the past.

A couple of generations ago, it was the fashion to take a real smooth swing and just patty-cake the ball around. The old school players used heavy drivers and let the club head do all the work. Today, not only are the courses longer, they are also getting tighter every year. So now a player has to be both powerful and accurate. Two prime examples of this modern player are, of course, Jack Nicklaus and Tom Weiskopf. It used to be that such a player was a freak, but I'm convinced that the player of tomorrow should model himself on them. To succeed, you had better have distance, accuracy, and all the shots. Just one of these qualities is no longer enough to make it to the top.

With these thoughts in mind, it's obvious that in the future there will be no place for a short, dinky swing, however accurate it may be. You just won't be able to compete with players who can reach the par-5's in two and take three or four clubs less than you do into long par-4's and par 3's. This, incidentally, is why today you can see a trend toward longer swings. Watch Nicklaus, Ben Crenshaw, Gary Player, Weiskopf, or myself; you'll see that at the top of the backswing all of us are swinging the club past parallel or at least to parallel.

Looking back on the major changes I have made in my own swing, I would have to say that they were motivated by the search for extra distance. Believe it or not, I used to have quite a short backswing before I went to Brigham Young University, and that old swing of mine was maybe a couple of inches flatter than the one I use today. I could hit irons that you wouldn't believe, better perhaps than I do now. If I hit a 5-iron ten feet off line that was a botched shot!

Accurate though I was, when I got to college I found that all the guys were outdriving me. I didn't like that too much, but more important I realized that I had to make some changes in order to get the ball out there a competitive distance. One guy in particular impressed me, and that was Mike Taylor, who was then the number one player on the team. He had this great, big upright swing. He would swing back high and full, and then drop down into the ball with his knees—and hit the ball a mile. Well, I just copied those elements of his swing.

I said earlier in this chapter that I was given every opportunity to succeed. Nowhere is that statement more true than in regard to the amount of time my dad spent with my practicing. Looking back on it now, I was fortunate in that he did make me practice as he did; by myself I doubt that I would have done it.

To me the interesting part of the game was always getting out there on the course and scoring the ball. I'm like Ben Crenshaw in that respect. Even today I will practice only if I'm playing poorly. If I'm playing well, I just go out and practice enough to keep it going.

As a junior I would play a lot during the day then in the evening I'd practice with my dad. Fortunately for me he was a really creative practicer. Perhaps he knew that just going through the bag would bore me very quickly. We did that, of course, but also he would have me hit a lot of shots around the green. He would also stick me in a lot of crazy lies. But it was good. I never got bored and kept right on practicing.

Another thing that Dad did for me was to ensure that I always had an immediate goal in front of me. Without goals, as a golfer, there's really no purpose to your play. Whether you want to be a professional one day or a good amateur player, you should set your ultimate goal and then break it down into steps. Then you just keep on improving so that you can take the next step up the ladder. At each stage in your development, you should judge yourself by your own performance—the kind of player you are, the good and the bad things. Don't ever judge yourself by what other people do, because you can't control that. All you can control is your own game.

To really improve, you have to be conscious of how good you really are at any one time. Then set your goal one step up the ladder and take it one step at a time. If you try to jump three rungs—if you are unrealistic about your game—you'll never get anywhere. For example, when a lawyer is fresh out of law school, he's not likely to win a case against a lawyer with twenty years' experience. And it's the same in golf. At each stage in your development, you've got to realize that there are people with more experience than you. You've got to be realistic and realize that they are ahead of you up the ladder.

Another point: To say you're the best, or that you have reached your potential, that's a bad state. I don't ever want to feel that I'm the best and that I'm not going to become any better. I just want to keep on improving, keep on eliminating mistakes. That's the best way to go, in my opinion. The guy who thinks he's got it made is the guy who goes nowhere.

Actually, the more you know, the more you feel you ought to know. In other words, your level of comprehension just keeps getting greater and greater. Some people say to me, "Gee, you're near the top and you're not going to be able to learn much more," but I think the more you learn the more you can see; your perspective is greater.

Progression is unlimited, thank goodness, otherwise golf wouldn't be much fun.

CHAPTER TWO

The Palm-to-Palm "Square" Grip

The fundamentals of a golf swing are like the foundations of a house; they must be laid on firm ground. My whole theory of golf is to get a good foundation, and then you can build as many stories on it as you want. In many cases developing a solid foundation requires change, specifically for people who have been playing a number of years in a way that feels good to them but with some basic flaw in their foundations that inhibits their growth as players.

Take someone who has a very strong grip, one of those "Harley-Davidson" jobs with four knuckles on the left hand showing, and the right hand as far under the grip as he can get it. Ask him why he grips that way and he'll reply, "Any other grip feels terribly weak to me." That may be true, but I tell you he's building his house on a shaky footing. As you will see a little later, he's doomed himself to fighting a hook, and a vicious hook at that. (You may wonder about the expression "Harley-Davidson" being applied to the grip—that's just my own description of a golfer with a very strong grip. When they waggle a club, they look just like one of those leather-jacketed cats revving up a powerful cycle. Very early Brando, and they last just about as long as players!)

Most people rebel against change because it requires self-sacrifice. But, if you want to be the best, you have to sacrifice. And if that means the total restructuring of your foundation, do it. The reward is progress as a golfer, which is a heck of a lot better than getting stuck at a certain level of proficiency and never improving.

I was fortunate that my father, when I first started, saw that I got a proper grip on the club. The grip is the first link in a series of chain reactions. If the hands are correctly positioned, the proper body muscles work in harmony to produce a position at impact that almost duplicates the address position.

What most golfers don't understand about the grip is that the easiest way to ensure square contact with the ball is to adopt a grip with which the palms of both hands are "square" with the target. This means that, if you took your grip, and then opened both hands, both palms would be at right angles or square to the target line, an imaginary line from the ball to the target.

The reason the square grip is best is because the hands will always tend to return to this palms-facing-target position at impact. Take a golf stance, and imagine a wall running through the ball at right angles to the target line. Now imagine that you are going to make a backhanded hit with an open hand against the wall. It would not matter what position you started the left hand in, because it instinctively returns to a position at impact in which the palm of the left hand is parallel to the wall. The same is true of the right hand. You instinctively "slap" the wall with the palm facing the wall.

The same principle applies when you have a golf club in your hands. If you set the clubface at right angles or square to the target, and your hands square to the target, the hands will instinctively return to this square position at impact. And you will have to make no compensations at all.

The same cannot be said for a strong grip, where, if you straightened your fingers, the palms would be tilted right, or a weak grip, where the palms would be tilted to the left. Assuming the clubface is square at address, and you take a strong grip, then the instinctive squaring up of the hands at impact will *close* the clubface at impact, unless you make a strong effort—a compensation in fact —to hold the clubface square. Similarly, with the weak grip, the tendency will be for the clubface to be open at impact. As a closed clubface will normally lead to a hook, or ball that curves to the left, and an open clubface, a slice, or a ball that curves to the right, let's agree that we can live without either!

Your hands are the only part of the body that put you in direct contact with the club. If they are badly positioned at the start, then your whole swing will be built around a fault and you will be making compensations in your swing forever. There is no easy way that you can consistently return the clubhead to "square" at impact. You have to start square to hit the ball square.

Back when I was in college, at Brigham Young, my grip, in terms of positioning, was about like Jack Nicklaus': my palms were turned a little to the right so that the V's created by the index finger and thumb pointed just right of my chin, which is the position most touring professionals favor. Today, my hands are, as I've said, what I call "square"—both palms square and both V's pointing to my chin. (Ben Hogan evolved to this grip.) Many technical experts would say this is, in terms of positioning, a "weak" grip. I'm not sure that I care for the terminology. If the palms of my hands were tilted to the left and the V's pointed to the left of my chin, which is a bad habit I fall into sometimes, then it would be a weak position. If the palms were tilted to the right and the V's pointed to the right of my chin, then that would be a strong position. But to me, if my palms are square and my V's point straight at my chin, this is square, and I think this is the best grip of all.

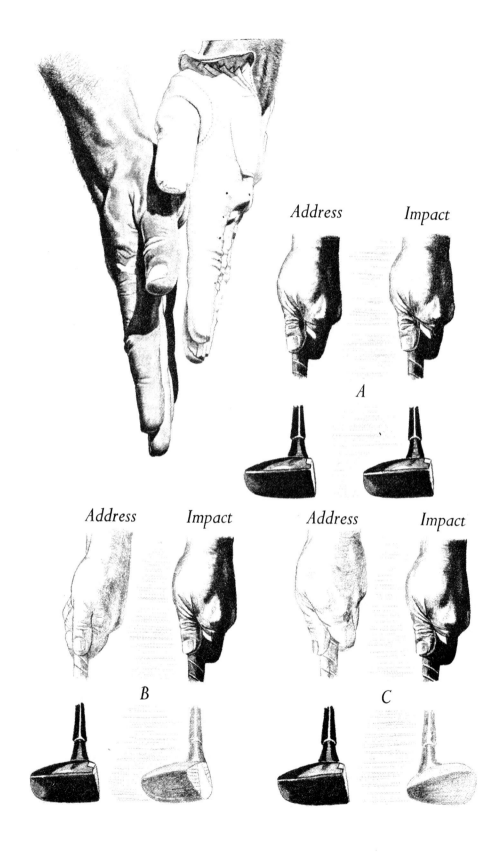

Address

Impact

A

Address

Impact

Address

Impact

B

C

THE VALUE OF THE VARDON GRIP

The grip that I have used from the beginning is the overlapping, or "Vardon," grip. In other words, the little finger of my right hand goes over and around the index finger of my left. I think this is the easiest and most proven way to hold a golf club. The ten-finger "baseball" grip spreads the hands too far apart for my liking, and there is a risk of their working independently instead of as a unit. Also, I've always felt the closer the hands are together the more clubhead speed you can achieve through the hitting area. The "interlocking" grip, where the little finger goes under and around the left index, has always felt and looked horrible to me. However, it does at least keep the hands unified.

I should add, however, that there are players who have achieved a high level of success using the ten-finger or interlocking grips. Art Wall and Bob Rosburg both use the "baseball" grip, and Jack Nicklaus has always used the interlocking. Usually, these grips are favored by golfers wtih shorter fingers than normal. The majority of players, however, tend to favor the overlapping. And I do too. I think it puts the fingers on the club the correct way and locks the hands together so that they work as one unit.

POSITIONING THE HANDS

In positioning the left hand on the grip, the grip must run across the middle joint of the left index finger, diagonally across the palm to a resting point under the muscle pad at the inner heel of

The most natural grip in golf is one where the palms of both hands face the target in what I term a "square" position. This is where the hands will instinctively return at impact. (A) You have to start square to hit the ball square. With your palms turned to the left initially, (B) the clubface will return to an open position at impact. (C) Turned to the right the instinctive "squaring" of the palms at impact forces the clubface to close.

the left hand. Your thumb should be placed so that it is at about the 12:30 mark on top of the grip. This is ideal. I don't recommend any more than 1 o'clock because this would cause you to rotate your hand out of a palm-facing, square position into a strong position.

The best way to find if the grip is positioned correctly in the hand is Ben Hogan's idea of leaving the thumb and the last three fingers off the shaft and lifting the club. As he put it: "Crook the forefinger around the shaft and you will discover you can lift the club and maintain a fairly firm grip on it by supporting it just with the muscles of that finger and the muscles of the pad and the palm." If the club were positioned too high, or too low, on the index finger, you'd be unable to lift the club up without its falling out of your hand.

Whereas the index finger plays its role in positioning, the little finger and the ring finger play their part in keeping the grip from moving around in the left hand during the swing. You always hear about pressure being applied in the last three fingers. I've always felt it's the last two. When pressure is applied in the last two, pressure in the third is automatic.

Once the grip is completed, the inverted V formed by the thumb and forefinger should point straight to the chin. Your palm will then be "square."

One of the most difficult points to get across in teaching is the matter of the grip pressure. You hear such things as "firm but not tight," but the problem with such expressions is that they mean different things to different people. I think I have found a good answer for the grip pressure in the left hand. It is this. *The grip pressure in the left hand should be as much as if you were swinging with your left hand alone.*

Try a few practice swings with your left hand and you will quickly establish the correct pressure for you. This is the pressure that enables you to control the club without gripping so tightly that you lose flexibility in the wrist.

(A) The club should run diagonally across the palm and come to rest under the muscle pad at the inner heel of the left hand. (B) Grip the club about as hard as if you were swinging with your left hand alone.

"Squaring" the Right Hand

Whereas the left-hand grip is largely a palm-finger grip, the right hand is solely a finger grip. The grip should run along the bottom joints of the fingers. Never allow the grip to slip down into the palm of the right hand. It makes for a looseness in the grip which allows the club to turn in the hands during the swing. A finger grip keeps the club in position at all times.

In my grip, I separate the index finger slightly from the rest. This finger, I feel, absorbs the shock of impact. Look at any good player's right index finger and it looks as though it's been fighting wars. This separation is largely a matter of choice; many good players prefer to keep all the fingers on the right hand grouped closely together. Although I advocate a slight separation, I'll leave the final choice to you.

I overlap my little finger by wrapping it between the knuckle of my left forefinger and my middle finger. I think this is the best way of overlapping. Some prefer to rest the little finger on top of the knuckle, but I've always felt this can create looseness in the grip.

When you fold your right hand over onto the left, you'll notice that your left thumb is totally accommodated by the hollow in the middle of your right palm; it fits right into the slot. A good checkpoint is that, if you can *ever* see your left thumb, your right hand grip is too strong.

When the grip is completed, the right thumb should rest on the left side of the shaft. The inverted V should then point to your chin.

One last word about pressure points in the right hand. There is a natural tendency to let the thumb drift away from the index finger, which creates a large gap. The club will tend to drop into the gap at the top of the backswing and waver around out of control. I therefore suggest slight pressure where the V is formed to keep the club solidly positioned in the right hand at the top.

Any other pressure in the hand should be applied in the little finger and the next two. The over-all pressure is slightly less than in the left hand. As Sam Snead once said, "Hold it like you were hold-

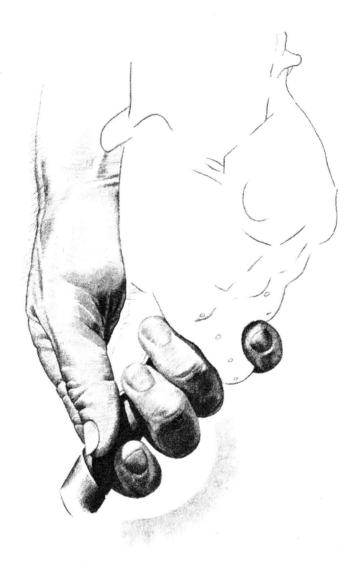

I prefer a slight separation between my right index finger and the rest. This finger absorbs the shock of impact.

ing a little bird." You will never see a long hitter grip the club tightly.

THE SQUARE GRIP AND OTHERS

There is no doubt that a lot of technical experts will criticize my advocating a "square" grip for average players. This doesn't worry me a bit. If I didn't think mine was the right way to grip a club, I wouldn't be using it now. I've tried gripping with my hands in both a strong and a weak position, but have evolved past either stage. My grip, I feel, is the most natural way to hold the club because it allows me to hit the ball either left to right or right to left. Back when I was in college, I used to hit a lot of hooks because I had a "stronger" grip. And when I fell into that problem of too weak a grip, I hit the ball to the right most of the time.

You can now see how important a good grip is. Not only does it affect the shot pattern, the way the ball curves in one direction or another; it also affects the trajectory, how high you hit your shots. Lee Trevino has a strong grip and, because of it, hits the ball extremely low. He hits the ball low because the club closes at the top of his backswing. Study any picture of Lee, at the top you'll see the clubface is dead shut, facing skyward. In comparison, mine is square and angled downward. I'm not going to go into a complicated discussion of the pluses or minuses of either position at this stage, but I want you to be aware of it because it proves the point about the whole swing being a chain reaction. You will see later the effect that either position, square or closed, has on a player's impact position.

So far I have mounted a verbal attack on the strong grip. What about a weak grip? First off, I rarely see average players with both their hands in too weak a position. I'll occasionally see someone with the left hand weak, and the right strong, or vice versa, but rarely with both hands in a weak position. Most average players adopt a strong grip because this way they feel so powerful they could tear up tree roots. A weak position gives a weak feeling, which is why so many people avoid it. As you can imagine, I don't advocate it.

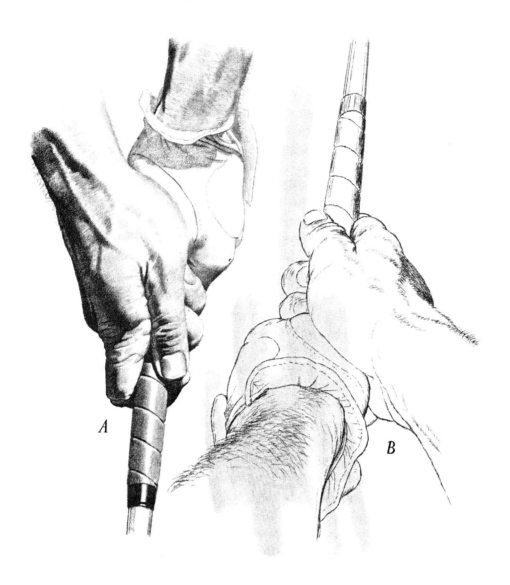

(A) The completed "square" grip. (B) A good checkpoint to ensure that both palms are square is that the V's formed by the index fingers and thumbs point directly to your chin.

You can see here the effect that the grip has on the swing. Lee Trevino has a strong grip and because of this at the top his clubface is closed and angled skyward. In comparison, mine is square and angled downward.

I would like to pick up on one point in the last paragraph. As I said, occasionally you'll see someone who has a "weak" left-hand grip, and a "strong" right-hand grip or vice versa. These are the worst grips in golf. Why? Because, first, the hands do not fit together properly with such grips, and so the hands cannot function as a unit. Second, and this really follows on from the first, the hands pull in opposite directions during the swing, which makes a sound action that much more difficult.

Of one thing I'm certain in the grip, the palms must face each other. By this I mean that if you take a correct grip, then straighten out your fingers, and slide the right hand up, both palms will face each other and touch at all points. That's why I like to call my grip a "palm to palm" grip, as well as being a "square" grip.

A good grip is essential in developing a repeating swing, hence my somewhat lengthy discussion on the subject. If you want to play golf, you've got to be prepared to spend time getting the "feel" of a good grip. For some, this will require patience. At first, any new grip will feel uncomfortable. It awakens muscles that weren't in use before. But allow yourself time to adapt. With patience you'll be amazed at how quickly you'll progress. Sometimes you have to take a step backwards in order to take two steps forward.

For the people who have doubts about a square grip, consider this: Ben Hogan, in his search for knowledge, took most of his life to discover what he termed a "weaker" grip (I call it a "square" grip) where the back of his left hand and the palm of his right hand faced the target. I, like many other people, am grateful for his discovery. I know that when I teach my children to play I'll teach them the "square," "palm to palm" grip.

CHAPTER THREE

Positioning, Posture and Plane

I remember playing in the Crosby at Pebble Beach in 1972. I had been pushing the ball to the right off the tee quite a bit, and couldn't figure out why. Late in the last round I caught sight of John Geertsen on the right side of the fairway. He made a motion with his hands, telling me to get my feet closer together. After this, I didn't hit another shot to the right.

At Doral, Florida, in 1975 I was having similar problems, although not quite as bad. In the first round I was leaving most of my iron shots to the right. It took me those two rounds to discover that my clubface was open at address. Before this I'd tried just about every swing conceivable to eliminate the problem. Instead of working on a cure I'd been working on the disease.

Hopefully, my experiences have shown you how much the address position affects the swing.

Every part of the body at address has a specific role to play. The feet, for example, are directors; they dictate which way the producer, the body, moves in the swing. The right foot must be set at right angles or "square" to the target line. This sets the right leg solid, which acts as a restricting point for the upper body to turn against, thus creating the necessary torque in the backswing. If the right foot were turned out, away from the target, I guarantee you would take the club back drastically inside the line, return like a wet noodle, forever, and never get torque. Conversely, if the right foot were turned in too much toward the target, the club would go back way outside the line, you'd get too much torque too soon and be unable to make a full backswing turn with your shoulders.

In addition to acting as a restricting point, the square right foot allows you to push the weight laterally back to the left side in the downswing. If your right foot were anywhere else but at right angles to the target line, you'd tend to push off in the wrong direction.

Tension may be a necessity in the right leg, but even the smallest amount of tension in the left leg will prove destructive to a free-swinging action. Flexibility in the left knee and leg muscles is a must. The left toe therefore should only be turned slightly outward, toward the target. This will create flexibility in the left knee and allow your hips and upper body to turn freely in both the backswing and the follow-through.

The distance the feet are spread apart is dictated solely by club selection. I, personally, play every shot from driver to sand wedge with the ball positioned off my left heel. Thus, the only foot that creates the width in the stance is the right. The left remains in line with the ball. I have never believed the theory that you play the driver off the left heel then gradually move the ball back in your stance toward the right foot, as many of the old teachers advocated.

The idea behind moving the ball back with the middle and short irons was to promote a steeper downswing arc. My feeling is, with the evolution of a more leg-oriented swing, the low point in the

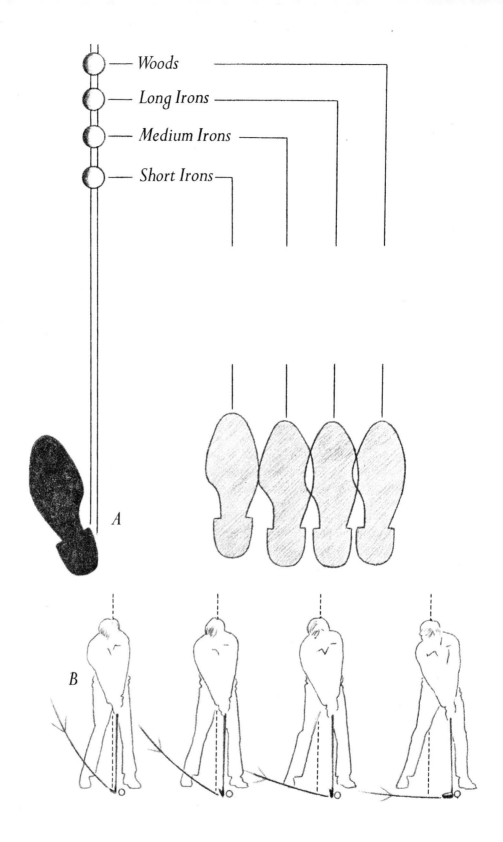

Woods

Long Irons

Medium Irons

Short Irons

A

B

swing, the place where the club reaches the base of the downswing area, has moved forward. Also, with the ball positioned in the middle of the feet, you only have one half of the body weight behind the ball. With the ball off the left heel, *all* the body weight is behind, especially the head, which is where the majority of the influencing weight rests. You've got twenty pounds upstairs and if you move your head in either direction, your weight automatically favors that side.

For a wood shot, I place my right foot just outside my right shoulder. You'll notice that each time you spread out the right foot to this width, your head lies to the right. This in itself creates the sweeping arc that is necessary on wood and long iron shots. As the right foot moves closer to the left, so your head becomes more centered over the ball. This by itself helps create a steeper downswing arc for the shorter irons.

I say keep it simple. Adopt just one ball position. That's enough for anyone to keep track of.

ALIGNMENT

The address position is like lining up a gun; if you don't have the target sighted, there is no way you'll hit the bull's-eye. If you're on target, it's simply a matter of pulling the trigger. I know, from experience, that if I'm off target something in my address is wrong.

When things go bad for me on tour, I often go down and see John Geertsen, who now lives in Monterey, California. Although he's in semiretirement, he still teaches at Monterey Peninsula Country Club, where his son, John, Jr., is the pro. John Geertsen is a fun-

(A) The ball is positioned off the left heel with every club, from driver to sand wedge. (B) The only foot that creates the width of stance is the right. As the right foot moves farther to the right, so the head does too. With the longer clubs this creates the necessary "sweeping" action by placing all the weight behind the ball.

damentalist and always has been. When I go down there, the last thing he'll tinker with is my swing. It's always my address position. I have the same faults over and over again. My stance might get too wide, my head could be too far behind the ball, my grip could be too weak, or the ball could be too far forward in my stance. These problems sound simple, but I can assure you that they do the most damage, and often it takes someone else to point them out.

When I first started, I was taught that everything should be parallel to the target line; feet, knees, hips, elbows, and shoulders. And I recommend this "square" alignment to you. It's the logical position for all but low-handicap players. Today, I am inclined to favor a slightly open position, where everything is aimed slightly to the left of the target. I have graduated to this open alignment mainly because it helps to promote a fade, which I feel is the easiest shot to control.

But there are other reasons. For example, standing open, you tend to retain a better perspective of the target line during the swing. Also, as you will see later in the book, you are forced to use the lower half of the body vigorously in the downswing. Any player who stands closed with the right foot back from the target line—and Billy Casper is a good example of this—will be forced to use his hands, arms, and upper body to get the club back to "square" at impact. His left side becomes a rigid obstacle, which restricts the leg action. Standing open, there is no obstacle and you have total freedom to use your legs.

At this stage, I must clear up a misconception. Many players think that an open stance means the left foot only is pulled back slightly away from the target line. This is not true. An open stance means *everything* is aimed slightly left of the target. Thus, the line across the toes (I call this the foot line) would point to the left of the target, and your knees, hips, and shoulders would then all be lined up parallel to the foot line. You must remember that I am talking now about a body alignment that promotes a shot that curves from left to right. For someone whose tendency has always been a right-to-left shot, an open stance is naturally harmful, and in this case I would recommend standing with everything parallel to or "square" to the target line. I never would advocate a closed stance, because, as I've explained, it promotes upper body rather than lower body action in the hitting area. The only way you can use this kind of motion effectively is to hit a very long hook all the time, like Casper.

Next we come to the most critical area of alignment: clubface positioning. Although the feet and body, I believe, are best aligned left of the target, the clubface should always be at right angles, facing the target, in a square position. You will see later, in the shot-making chapter, that this rule applies on any shot.

GETTING THE JUMP ON POSTURE

Sometimes, especially when I'm playing well, I feel much like a cougar would when he's ready to spring on his prey; as though I could jump ten feet in the air from a standing start. This alive, catlike mobility is created by an even distribution of my weight, between the heel and the ball of each foot; by a comfortable flex in my knees and by having my butt out behind my heels. In essence, it's just like I'm about to jump, not forward or back, but *straight up in the air*. Develop this feeling and in my opinion you will have taken the first step in developing perfect posture.

To help ingrain the feeling, stand with your feet shoulder width apart and your arms hanging naturally at your sides. Now, as if you were going to jump straight up in the air, flex your knees. Do not bend the knees, flex them. Notice your weight is distributed evenly between the heels and the balls of your feet, and that the over-all feeling is solid, one of readiness.

Even the best players sometimes fall into a habit of positioning their weight too much toward the toes or too far back on their heels. Either way creates problems.

You can imagine if your weight initially were forward, on the balls of your feet, what would happen in the backswing; your weight going back to the heels would cause your body to move back away

35

from the ball. Similarly, if the weight started on the heels and moved to the toes in the downswing, you'd fall forward toward the ball. I have fallen into the problem of having my weight on my heels several times and found that I lose my balance in the follow-through and have a tendency to hit a lot of hooks or shots straight right.

Keeping this "jumping" image in mind gets my weight positioned properly, between the heels and the toes. I would add, however, that there should be a minor distribution of weight toward the inside of the feet. The last thing you want to be is flat-footed with your feet locked solidly on the ground. You get the weight to the insides of the feet by turning the knees slightly inward, toward one another. This strengthens your foundation. You may remember that earlier I discussed the purpose of setting the foot at right angles to the target line, namely to create a restricting point for the upper body to turn against. Having the right knee kicked slightly in adds to this purpose; it braces the right leg so that it acts in the swing in the same way as a gatepost would for a gate. First, the right leg will then provide a fixed point for the upper body to turn around. Second, it prevents lateral movements of the hips, or what is commonly called a sway. And, third, it helps to restrict the hip action and helps create the necessary torque between the upper and lower body.

There are players on the tour who prefer to have their legs bowed outward instead of turned inward. Supposedly this is a powerful position, but in my opinion it allows an unnecessary amount of movement. Any player who has the knees bowed out will be inclined to sway like a tree in a breeze; the backswing has no fixed turning point and no restriction. This may provide an extra few

(A) With good posture, you should feel as if you can "spring" straight up in the air. (B) To find the correct distance you should be from the ball, hold the club straight out in front of you, then let the head fall to the ground. (C) In the completed address my weight is evenly distributed between the heel and ball of each foot, the knees are comfortably flexed, and my butt is out behind my heels.

A

B

C

yards off the tee, but it cannot be conducive to accuracy. The right leg supports and restricts the backswing turn, the left side supports the thrust of the downswing and the follow-through. Were the turn unrestricted in either direction, the swing would become a "jellyfish" type motion, wobbly and unco-ordinated.

I'm often asked about the correct distance to stand from the ball. My answer is simple: Your posture dictates the distance. Here's how it works.

Stand erect, feet comfortably apart. Next, form your grip on the club and hold both arms out fully extended. Assume the "jump" position that I showed you a minute ago, butt out behind your heels, knees slightly flexed. Now just let the weight of the clubhead fall to the ground, taking your arms and upper body along with it. Notice that you have arrived in a position where your arms remain comfortably extended. Your back is not rounded, but fairly straight. There you not only have the correct posture, but you are also the correct distance from the ball.

ANGLING THE WRISTS

If I were going to punch someone with my left hand, I would do it with the wrist in a straight anatomical position. There would be a slight angle at the outside of the left wrist between the outside of the left forearm and the back of the left hand. If the wrist were bowed at the joint (convex) or very much concave, undoubtedly I'd break it. This straight anatomical position is the strongest position in golf, as it is in boxing.

Over the years keeping the hands ahead of the ball has been heavily stressed. Unfortunately, many have taken this advice and misinterpreted it. The farther you put your hands forward, the more the left wrist is inclined to bow outward toward the target. I explained earlier what happens at the top of the backswing with a strong grip. "Bowing" has the same effect—you arrive at the top of the swing *dead shut.*

I recommend that the hands be in front of the ball, but only slightly, mind you; the top of the grip should be level with the front of the ball. This is far enough forward to prevent the right hand from getting "snatchy"; that is, pulling the club back too fast in the take-away. But this is done in a way that keeps the left wrist in the straight anatomical position, so that a slight angle is created in the back of the left wrist. This angle, as you will see later, must remain constant in the backswing for you to arrive in a "square" position at the top.

While we're on the subject, there is another very important angle of the wrists which is apparent when you look at a golfer from the side, in other words, behind the ball looking toward the target. If you study this position, you'll notice that the wrists are slightly arched. This is important because only when the wrists are arched do the hands and arms work in one piece and in the correct plane when the club is drawn back away from the ball.

The most common error is that the golfer sets his hands so low that a large angle is formed between the left hand and forearm. This puts your hands into a position where they dominate the swing and force an unnatural swing plane. The other extreme—pushing the hands so high that a straight line is formed by the left arm and club shaft—is less common but just as damaging.

Carefully study the slight arching of my wrists in the illustration and try to duplicate it yourself. One of the best aids in this regard is a full-length mirror. Take your address and then check it in the mirror. You can adjust your wrists, if necessary, to the correct position.

Like all the other parts of the body, the elbows also have their part to play. However, one thing that is important to realize is that the position you adopt most naturally with both elbows is largely a result of the grip you take.

If you take a very strong grip on the club with both hands turned to the right from the square position, you will find that the left elbow tends to move clockwise and face toward the target; it will also move away from your body. Your right elbow will tuck

(A) The grip of the club is aligned with the front of the ball. (B) Only when the wrists are slightly "arched" do the hands and arms work in one piece and in the correct plane.

down, very close to your right hip. Now take a backswing from this address position. You will note that the tendency is to swing very much inside the target line, low and around the body in what would be described technically as a very flat plane. This is obviously undesirable.

Now adopt an extremely weak grip. See how the left elbow now tends to turn counterclockwise and moves closer to the body. And the right arm will tend to straighten and move farther away from the body. Again, take a backswing from this position. The tendency is to swing back outside the swing line and in a very upright plane. This again is an obviously undesirable extreme.

Now adopt the square grip I have been recommending to you. You will note that the left arm is in a comfortable position with the left elbow pointing in the general direction of the left hip. This is fine. However, if you're not careful you will note that the right elbow tends to be away from the body, and, from this position, you could start the swing outside the line. Worse, the right elbow tends to be too straight—although not as straight as with the weak grip—and this could lead to a "flying right elbow" at the top instead of the proper action, where the right elbow folds on the backswing.

Even with the proper "square" grip, you do have to consciously manipulate the right elbow a little at address so that this necessary folding action takes place naturally while going back. By the way, anyone who adopts a square grip will have this problem. Ben Hogan had this tendency, so does Gary Player. So do I, and so will you. But the solution is not difficult even though it will seem a little awkward at first. Without disturbing your square grip, drop your right shoulder slightly and gently push the right elbow down an inch or so. This will give you the correct position of the elbow to enable you to take the club straight back from the ball on the swing line for the first foot or so, and then up into the correct swing plane. This ideal swing plane will be in between the very flat or very upright.

YOUR ADDRESS SETS THE PLANE

I think that this would be a good time to get into swing plane in a bit more detail.

Basically, it is my contention that your build largely determines how you stand to the ball and thus determines the plane of your

Your build will largely determine how you stand to the ball and your swing plane. A tall person, like myself, will naturally adopt an upright plane because I bend from the waist and hold my hands lower than a shorter person. An an example, Gary Player bends less from the waist, holds his hands higher, and thus has a flatter swing plane.

swing. A taller person like myself tends to adopt a more upright plane quite naturally. This is because I bend from the waist more and hold my hands lower at address than a shorter person, like Gary Player, for example. Gary bends less from the waist, holds his hands higher and therefore has a flatter swing plane than I do.

There is a lot to be said for an upright swing plane. When the club is swung in an upright plane, the club does not have to come inside the swing line very much on the backswing. By staying close to the swing line throughout the swing, your margin of error is reduced compared to a flat swing plane where the club comes into the ball from much farther inside the swing line, and thus will stay on line a shorter distance through the hitting area.

However, as I've said, your basic swing plane is pretty much forced on you by your build. If I stood as erect as Gary does, then my hands would be so high off the ground I would have to use super-long clubs to reach the ground. The clubs would actually be too long for me to control. If Gary were to bend from the waist as much as I, then he would have to use super-short clubs. He would achieve an upright swing plane but, due to the short clubs, would generate very little power.

Personally I feel that too much has been made of this matter of swing plane. If you stand up to the ball as I have suggested, you will have taken the first step toward creating the right swing plane for your build. And, as you will see later in the book, I have a simple swing key that will enable you to keep the club on the correct track during the swing.

CHAPTER FOUR

Setting the Pattern
of Address

Watch any good player hit a few shots during a competitive round and you'll see that he has a set pattern of actions, from the time he arrives at the ball, to the time he begins his swing. This machine-like pattern doesn't, or shouldn't, change, even under extreme pressure.

Some players incorporate into the pattern the same gestures over and over again. Charlie Coody is a good example. Charlie gets to the ball, checks his card for yardage, then tosses some grass in the air to find out which way the wind is blowing. And he does this even when there is no wind! It's all part of a system. Bert Yancey said that he once put a stopwatch on most of the best tour players to find out exactly how long it took each to go through his individual pattern. My elapsed time from taking the club out of the bag to starting the backswing was fifteen seconds on each shot. He said the elapsed time on all the players was so close from shot to shot it was scary. In other words, most good players are so used to doing the same things over and over again they've become like robots.

If you ever see me play you'll notice that I have a pattern that is set at a fairly deliberate pace. I go through my routine regardless of whether I'm hitting a driver, an iron, or even a putter. My pattern of address forces me to be deliberate and allows me time to calculate and process the elements of the shot I'm about to play. It ensures that my mind remains focused on the key fundamentals we discussed earlier in the book, such as alignment of the clubface and the body, the distance I stand away from the ball, and correct positioning of the ball off my left heel. All this is automatic. And probably the biggest advantage is that my mind remains intent on positive action. I have no time to think where the ball *could* go, but I am constantly thinking about where I *want* the ball to go. I know, whenever I deviate from my pattern, I'm opening the door to a whole bunch of unwelcome negative thoughts as well as running the risk of ruining my rhythm and timing by rushing the shot.

I'm sure you will get a clearer picture of what I mean when I say "pattern" if I take you through the sequence of steps. However, I offer mine only as a possible guide to developing your own. And I don't, by any means, say that mine is the best. For now it is the best that I can devise. Here it is:

1. I stand behind the ball, with the club held loosely in my left hand, to get a clear picture of the target line.
2. Keeping the target line clearly in focus, I move diagonally to the left to a point at right angles to the target line through the ball.
3. Here I turn, adopt my grip, step toward the ball with my right foot leading, and at the same time take a half swing.
4. The clubface is placed on the ground behind the ball "square" to my intended target, while both feet are placed together.
5. I spread my left foot so the ball is set off my left heel. My right foot is then spread according to the club I'm hitting.
6. At this stage, I go into "constant motion," shuffling my weight

45

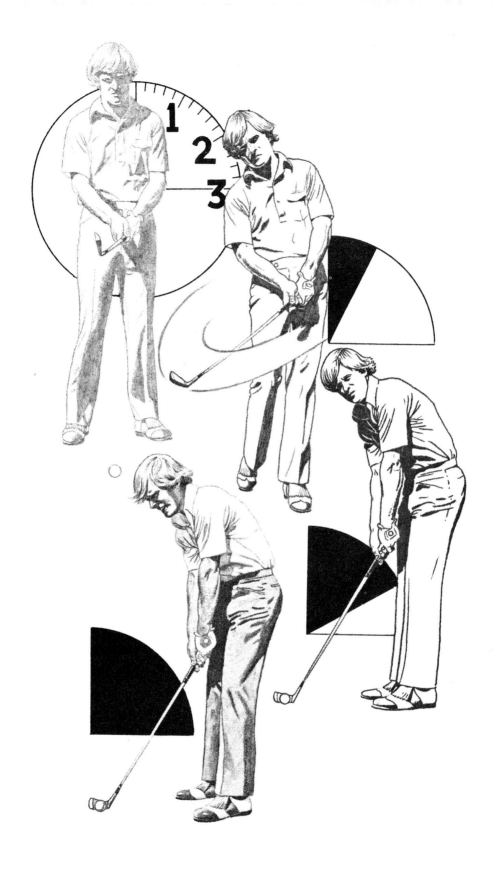

from side to side by picking my feet up. At the same time I am waggling the club (mine is not a conventional waggle, as I'll explain in a minute) and looking at the target. I look at the target and waggle four times, then initiate my swing with a rocking forward of my weight to the left side and then back to the right side, an action initiated by my knees.

There you have the procedure. Needless to say, I left out most of the calculating and computing that goes on during the course of the setup routine. We'll go into this later in the book.

There are a couple of things I do in my pattern that most others don't. For example, I place my feet together, then spread them apart. Many pros step into the ball with their right foot first, then without ever putting their feet together, spread the left foot and then the right. I feel that this method makes proper alignment too much a matter of chance. My method, on the other hand, not only ensures that I get the ball lined up with my left heel, but also makes certain that my feet and body are parallel to the target line. If you put your feet together, you'll see how easy it is to line up the rest of your body. In fact, it's almost instinctive.

You noticed, I'm sure, that I made no mention of a practice swing. I don't believe in practice swings. Any swing I take before hitting a shot is in my mind, and thus I conserve physical energy. Besides, a golf swing is built largely on muscle memory. So, if you make a bad practice swing, which often happens, because there is a tendency to swing haphazardly, then it's likely you'll do the same to the ball. A waist-high half swing is as close as I ever come to a practice swing. It is just enough to give me the feel of the shot I'm about to hit as well as relieve any tension I may have in my wrists and

My address pattern: 1) I stand behind the ball. 2) I move diagonally to a point at right angles to the target line. 3) I adopt my grip, step in, and take a half swing. 4) Square the clubface and place both feet together. 5) Spread my left foot then my right. 6) Go into constant motion. The whole process takes fifteen seconds.

hands. There are, in fact, very few pros on the tour who take practice swings; Tom Shaw, Herbert Green, and Kermit Zarley are the only notable exceptions I know of.

Unlike most pros, I don't waggle the club, either. Instead, I have what could be called a "lift and look" type action. I lift the club so that it is suspended over the ball for a second, and look at the target at the same time. Then as my eyes look from the target to the ball, the club drops back to the earth again behind the ball. I repeat this procedure four times.

During this time I remain in "constant motion." I was taught early in my career that no player gets anywhere standing up to a golf ball like a statue. You've got to be alive, like a boxer about to throw a punch; otherwise you've got no chance. This is why I keep my weight moving from side to side. I almost get a running start on the swing, and this makes the transition from a static position into the swing that much easier.

The last move, and an integral part of my pattern, is the triggering device, the initiating move. As the period of constant motion ends, the second after my right foot returns to earth, I trigger the swing by rocking a slight amount of my weight first to my left side and then back to my right. This is done with my knees and involves, simply, a kicking inward of the right knee and the reverse with the left. Incorporated is a movement forward of the hands—very slight and almost unnoticeable except to the trained eye—that is induced by the knee action. This is described technically as a forward press. Although this is not something I'm conscious of, the smooth transition in the lower body into the swing is created by the rocking forward, then back, of the knees. The smoothness in the upper body is created by a slight forward and backward movement of the hands. I repeat: if you trigger the swing with your knees, the forward press in your hands becomes automatic.

There is one other point I would like to make about my pattern of taking address, and it concerns the initiating move, the "rock forward, rock back" action. This is not just a personal idiosyncrasy of mine. It serves a very necessary function. If you stand up to the ball with your weight evenly distributed and try and go straight into your backswing, you'll find it very awkward. Or if you stand up to the ball with your right knee kicked in a little, which puts a little more weight on the left foot than the right, and try to swing back from there, it's even more awkward. And there's a very good reason for the awkward feelings in both cases. To execute the backswing, the weight must be placed on the right foot, and not the left. The easiest way to get your weight to the right foot is to do it as a recoil action, a "forward then back" action. The right knee triggers the rock forward by flexing inward toward the left. As the right knee starts to flex back, it draws the whole left side into motion.

CHAPTER FIVE

Principles of the Modern Swing

There's not a golfer in the world who doesn't desire—to a greater or lesser extent—to have a fine golf swing. And yet it's a fact that the vast majority of players are double-figure handicappers or worse. There has to be a reason for that.

Although lack of practice may account for some of the funny swings one sees around, I know that it can't be the reason for a lot of them. Just go to your friendly neighborhood driving range and walk down the line of golfers. Out of a hundred golfers pounding out balls, I'll bet that you'll see only one really good swing, and maybe half a dozen pretty good swings. The rest are bad!

I am convinced that the real reason most swings don't improve is that these golfers have no clear idea of how they swing—if they did, many would no doubt have a rude awakening! It's equally apparent they have no true visual picture in their minds of how they *should* swing. As I look back on the way I started in the game, I can see how fortunate I was. Not just that I started at an early age, or that I had the most dedicated of fathers to help me. It was the *way* that Dad started me that was important, and that is relevant here.

When I started, Dad had Ben Hogan's and Sam Snead's books and he formulated ideas from them. Although he had never had a lesson himself, he would literally imitate their moves in front of a mirror and then he'd have me imitate the moves in front of the full length mirror that we had in the basement. By looking at the pictures in the book, I could see what a good golf swing should look like. Then, I would swing looking in the mirror and I could see for myself how close I was getting.

In some cases, I could see what needed work, and in others Dad would point out where I was going wrong. It is really great having someone to watch you, because when you're starting out you have no idea sometimes what the heck you're doing. You can't swing and see yourself at the same time.

Incidentally, that is one of the great values of going to a teaching professional. He knows the swing, and from experience his eyes are trained to spot instantly deviations from good form. The only problem with lessons is that, again, you can't see yourself. That's why I am convinced the ideal way to learn is to have a fine pro *and* a TV instant replay machine. Any means whereby you can see yourself.

Pictures of the correct swing and your own swing are the key to relating to your subconscious. Then when you program thoughts into your head they are realistic thoughts and not something you *think* you are doing or think you should be doing. So many people— professionals and amateurs alike—think they swing perfectly when in fact their swings are terrible. And the reason is: *They have never seen themselves swing!*

The eye is a great deceiver and many times what you think you are and what you really are are two quite different things. It's like the first time you hear your voice on a tape recorder. You say, "Gee, is that really me?" O.K., so the two main factors in learning the swing are, first, to get a true visual picture of how you swing, and, second, to get a true visual picture to implant into your subconscious of how you want to swing.

As regards the first objective, the ideal way is to have a video-tape replay machine and a professional for his knowledge and ability to analyze the swings recorded. However, there are other ways, which don't involve that kind of investment in equipment. For instance, many families today have movie cameras. Even the simplest movie camera can give you a good idea of what your swing really looks like.

Even better, of course, are the more expensive models offering slow motion. And if you have a movie camera with an adjustable shutter, then you can also get stop motion to sharpen individual frames.

You don't have a movie camera? No problem. I'm sure you have some sort of still camera or have a friend who has one. If you can lay your hands on a camera with a top shutter speed of 1/500 of a second or faster, you're in business. With very little practice you can get the individual pictures you need of the swing. Of course, if you have a Polaroid camera, you will see immediately if you have the pictures needed. However, even if you are using conventional film, you will get a pretty good sequence if you take enough shots.

Last, but by no means least, don't forget the value of a big, full length mirror. This not only lets you see how you are swinging, but also is useful in training yourself to incorporate a new move into your swing.

Moving to the second objective—getting a true visual picture of the correct swing to implant into your subconscious—many of the techniques we have just discussed will help. When you make a really good swing and have recorded it on TV tape or film, this image of *you* swinging well is going to help you program good swings in the future.

However, there are other ways and we are going to use them

52

all in this section on the swing. First, of course, we are going to use words to describe the correct golf swing. We are also going to use words to clear up misconceptions about the golf swing. These misconceptions cause a lot of confusion among average golfers, and if you're confused mentally about your objectives, you're going to formulate confused visual images of the swing.

This brings up another point. Your body responds to visual images. So, when you've read a piece of written instruction I give, immediately translate it into a visual image for your body to respond to. With regard to the illustrations, you don't need to translate them as they are visual images already. However, I would really urge you to make the fullest possible use of them. They have been carefully selected to show you visually the key moves in the golf swing. If you apply them to *your* golf swing, I know you will progress quickly. Remember, I speak from experience: When I was growing up, I used the fine swings of Sam Snead and Ben Hogan for such study. And my swing today is largely a result of this effort.

First of all, I'm going to discuss some over-all concepts of the swing. Then, we'll move to a thorough review of the swing in detail. In the course of these discussions I'll point out along the way some of the more common misconceptions about the swing, including some concepts I consider to be outdated. Following this, I'm going to isolate and discuss what I consider to be the five basic moves in the golf swing; the moves that make it all happen. Finally, we'll discuss the difference between working on your swing in practice and using the swing on the course.

THREE MAJOR CONCEPTS

Take any athletic action and it involves a shifting of the weight. If you throw a ball, you can wind up properly only if you place your weight on your right foot. The windup has to be made with the weight on the right foot. When you throw the ball, or hit the baseball, where's the weight? On the *left* foot. Without this back and forth shift of the weight, you cannot develop power. Just try a throwing action and force your feet and legs to remain still, and you will see what I mean. The ball would go nowhere, in terms of distance.

It's the same in golf. You have to wind up in the backswing with the weight on the right foot. In the downswing, the weight must shift to the left foot in order to release the power built up by the windup. The only difference in golf is that the ball is stationary, and this means keeping the feet in place. This in turn means that the shifting of the weight in golf has to be accomplished primarily by knee action. (Illustrations on the swing follow page 64.)

To demonstrate this to yourself, stand up and put your feet about shoulder width apart, with your weight evenly distributed between your feet. Now put more weight on your right foot than on your left. Study what happened. Your left knee popped out in front of you. Now shift your weight to your left foot; your right knee popped forward. That, in a nutshell, is the weight shift in golf. It's all in the knees.

The second concept is the correct use of the body and arms to provide power. And here I immediately want to dispose of one idea that has been around a long time—too long, in my opinion. This is the proposition that the swing is entirely left-sided or left-side controlled. Both sides of the body have their role to play. The left side turning against the right leg is what gives you the coiling action in the backswing. But meanwhile, the right side is hardly passive, as is commonly taught. The right side winds up in combination with the weight shift to the right foot in a very similar manner to throwing a ball. In the downswing, the left side does lead with a strong, backhanded pulling action. But it is the release of the right arm aided by a strong thrust of the right leg that provides most of the power. The left side only pulls, whereas the right side provides the force.

The third concept is that it is the hands, wrists, and forearms that enable you to control the way the clubface points and thus the direction on the shot. The easiest way to demonstrate the correctness of this is at the address position. Take your address position and then look down at your hands. First, turn your hands, wrists, and forearms to the right in a clockwise motion. Now study what happens to the clubface; it is open. If you did this in the backswing and didn't make a compensating action in the downswing, the result would be a slice. Similarly, if you turned your hands, wrists, and forearms to the left in an anticlockwise motion, the club would close and would lead to a hook unless some compensating move were made. Now return to the address and lift the club by bending the wrists straight up. That's the only type of action your wrists should make in the swing.

Before I go into a detailed explanation of the swing, I think it would be as well to explain my purpose here. It is this. You have to understand the various parts of a swing to be able to put it all together. In the same way that an auto mechanic must have a thorough understanding of an engine before he takes it apart—otherwise he will never get it back together again—so must you understand the working parts of a golf swing.

The Swing

As I said earlier, in the section on setting the pattern for address, I initiate my swing by a "rock forward, rock back" move of my knees. This gets my weight set on the inside of my right foot so that I am ready to start the swing.

The first move away from the ball is a nice flowing action with everything going away together. If you watch the guys with classic swings, the guys who have lasted a long time in this game, like Sam Snead and Julius Boros, you will notice that their takeaway is a relaxed, lazy type of move where everything moves from the ball in one piece. This is the most natural type of takeaway because nothing is forced.

Although the body action and hand action blend together, for the sake of clarity I'm going to discuss them separately.

First, let's discuss the action of the lower body. Right off, there should be no lateral movement in the hips. They should turn just as though they were in a barrel. What makes it look as though fine players make a lateral move is the action of the knees. As I said earlier, you rock your knees forward and back so as to shift the weight to the right foot, and this one-two action of the knees does give the appearance of a lateral move in the hips. But it is an illusion. The right hip in reality just turns straight back behind the player. You can only move laterally, approximately one to two inches before your right side breaks down and you sway.

I think it was Percy Boomer, in his book *On Learning Golf*, who first came up with this "barrel" image for the hips. And for my money it is still the best way to go. It prevents any hint of lateral sway in the hips, but it also is a beautiful image to impress on you the importance of keeping the hips *up* in stable position.

Put another way, you don't want your knees bending at any point in the swing any more than they were at address. This extra bending of the knees is quite common and it does give an illusion of power. In reality, however, if the knees bend more, the hips and whole body have to drop down with them. Then, in the downswing you'll have to make a compensating move upwards. Enough said. Let's keep it simple. The hips should turn in place.

Turning to leg action in the backswing, I think it fair to say that you won't have much problem with your left leg as long as you get it moving with everything else at the start of the swing. The turn of the hips will pretty much pull the left leg into the desired position at the top. However, the same cannot be said for the right leg.

I said when describing the address position that you must set up the right leg solidly so that it acts like a fixed gatepost for the swing to turn around. True, it rocks forward and back a little before the swing starts, but once it comes back from the forward press the right knee has to be set solid in the same position it was in at address. There must be no lateral movement of the leg, and only a little backward movement toward the rear as the hips pull on the upper leg. You should feel great resistance in the muscles of the thigh. If you don't feel such resistance, then your hips will keep on turning like a wet noodle and you will never develop torque between the turn of the upper body and this resistance in the right leg.

The resisting action of the right leg is what prevents excessive hip turn. Many women golfers, and some men, too, make that "no resistance" mistake. Then the hips will turn almost as much as the shoulders because the right leg hasn't done its work—it has been allowed to collapse and just pivots around with the right hip. You can't get any power this way.

An image that may help you is that the right leg is in effect the foundation stone of the backswing. It's set solid and you simply turn your shoulders as fully as possible against the resistance in the foundation. And that in essence is the coil.

And here I want to go on record as not going along with the theory that the order of movement in the backswing should be hands, arms, shoulders, with the hips, left leg, and foot being dragged away late in the backswing by the turn of the shoulders. In other words, I would get to the top having tremendous coil and finally the left foot would rise. There is too much tension in that type of swing for my taste. I believe that for longevity—for a swing like Snead's or Boros'—you should use limited tension. The only tension I feel is through the left side of my back and then only at the top of the backswing. Essentially, I just try to plant the right leg firmly, and let the left side move right by it. I try to keep my left side as relaxed as possible until the top of the swing, where you will get some tension in the left side of your back because your body turn and range of motion stop. (Actually, the tension is felt in the latissimus dorsi muscle, commonly called the "lat muscle." It works like a slingshot. You pull it back and then release it, getting an automatic return and speed through the ball.) I have found that golfers who don't allow their left heel to lift until last or don't move their left side in the first movement of the backswing build a snatchy type of swing. It may have tremendous coil because of the restriction on the hips, but they shorten the backswing and they lose something I consider just as important as coil, namely rhythm. Rhythm comes from a swinging action of the club, rather like the swing of a pendulum. To my mind you must have both—a swinging action amplified by coil.

I also don't like much what is called "extension" in the back-swing. When you go for too much extension—the distance the club-head travels away from the body—and try to keep the clubhead as low to the ground as possible in the take-away, you create an unnaturally wide arc that is extremely hard to time and control. You also become too clubhead oriented. Your mind is focused on getting the clubhead as far from your body as possible and on nothing else. Since it is a manufactured move and not a natural one, it requires the golfer to practice very hard to maintain it. There's also a real danger of extending so far that it pulls the head off the ball to the right, in other words, a sway.

I prefer a much more natural action, as follows: The "rock back" action of the knees from the forward press starts the whole of the upper body—shoulders, arms, hands, and club back in one piece. Having got the weight slightly to the inside of the right foot, the right arm and shoulder then go into a perfectly natural action almost exactly like the windup for throwing a ball. The right arm pulls back and folds, and with the right arm pulled back and up, the left arm counters with a natural stretching action. This natural action in the left arm, a stretching, thrust-down action, sets up the leverage action between the two sides of the body by which the club is carried to the top of the swing.

Actually, the natural stretching action of the left arm is what good golfers feel when they are playing well, and is actually the cause of all the talk about extension. However, it is a mistake to think of *making* the left arm extend way out from the body. It will extend far enough quite naturally if the right arm is allowed to function naturally. The right-arm "pull up" action *induces* the left-arm stretch. Also, as long as your shoulders turn, you will have good extension. Your left arm will only break down if your shoulders prematurely stop turning.

Another reason why extension for the sake of extension is bad is that, according to its proponents, you should delay the cocking of the wrists until the last part of the backswing. Again, this is an unnatural move, and anything that is unnatural will need a lot of work to keep in shape.

What should happen is that, as the right arm pulls back and up and the left arm stretches, this sets up a natural leverage action between the hands, and this will induce the wrists to cock much earlier than the "not before waist high" advice of the extension merchants.

One of the best ways to convince yourself that an earlier cocking action of the hands is natural is to swing the club with one hand at a time. If you try with the left hand alone, you'll find that your left wrist is starting to cock before the left hand ever gets past the right hip in the backswing. And the same will occur if you try to swing the right hand alone. The right wrist starts to cock very early in the backswing. If you find this earlier wrist break natural when swinging with one hand, doesn't it make sense that it is the logical and natural way to go when swinging with both hands?

In making this comparatively early wrist break, or early set, as it is sometimes called, I want to again remind you that it is the hands and wrists that control the squareness of the clubface or otherwise in the swing. You set up with that slight angle in the back of the left wrist at address. You maintain that angle as you make the wrist break. There must be no twisting of the left wrist clockwise or anticlockwise, otherwise you are opening or closing the clubface, leading respectively to a slice or a hooking action. Let your shoulders do the turning!

Of course, it is possible to hit the ball straight from an open (slice) or shut (hook) position, but somewhere in the swing you will have to compensate by turning the wrists the opposite way, or by moving your body or head, in front of the ball. Some players even fall back, leave their weight on the right side, and close the clubface. This, as I have said, makes the golf swing too complicated.

A good image I have used to help me feel the square "straight up" wrist break is to imagine that, once I have my left wrist in the correct position at address, it is cast in steel so that there's no way I can break the wrist other than square. I repeat: A square golf swing is never changing the relationship of the left wrist that you had at address.

The "square" wrist break is so important, and so few people understand it. I think what complicates it for most people is that the wrist break occurs when the shoulders and hips have started their turn. That's why I like to explain it at the address position. It gets rid of these complicating factors.

There are other advantages of the early wrist break that I would like to point out. The earlier you break the wrists, within reason, the more time you have to set the clubface in that set square position. You have more time to feel where the club and clubface are. The other point is that the early set tends to make you release the wrists later in the downswing, the "late hit," as it is often called. A very early set would only start to release in the downswing, approximately one foot from the ball, whereas a later set would be initiated at hip level. I think the best method is somewhere in between. In contrast, the advocates of extension and the late wrist break never know where their clubface is going to land up until near the top of the backswing, where the club is traveling much faster than in the take-away. This makes the "late set" of the wrists, as we might call it, that much more difficult to execute. Also, breaking the wrists pretty much as the last action in the backswing encourages the wrists to uncock as the first move of the downswing. Young, strong professionals *can* get away with this move because of their tremendously strong leg action into the downswing. But if they didn't use the legs very strongly, they would "cast" or throw from the top. The average golfer, both man and woman, usually doesn't have strong leg action, or at least not as strong as the touring pro. So his or her chances of saving a late wrist break by strong leg action are almost nil.

Ironically, both Jack Nicklaus and Gary Player both use the "extension, late wrist break" backswing. This, I feel, is a learned move as opposed to a relaxed, natural one. But before you emulate them, I would beg you to consider just how strong and talented they are and the amount of practice they devote to their games.

Having broken down the actions of the backswing, now let's get into positioning at the top of the swing.

First, your weight will be slightly on the inside of your right foot and the hips will have turned as fully as possible consistent with keeping the right knee in place. The shoulders will have turned to their maximum, and the hands and the club will be over the right shoulder. In fact if you let go of the club it would strike the point of the right shoulder. Another key that the backswing has been executed properly is that the club will point right at the target like an arrow. Your right arm and hand are in the cocked, "windup for the throw" position, and your left arm is still stretching. And, I will say it again, the angle in your left wrist is exactly the same as it was at address.

While we're here at the top, I want to pick up a point that I made at address. As I said then, I think the swing plane you adopt is pretty much a product of your build. But the secret of getting the right swing plane for *you* is first setting up correctly and then this right-handed "windup for the throw" action. If you do the windup with the right arm correctly, your hands will land up at the top of the swing with the club's shaft pointing over the tip of your right shoulder. Another way of saying the same thing is that, if you aim to have your hands pointing the shaft over your right shoulder toward the target at the top of the swing, you will be in the right swing plane. It's that simple.

Extending the thought a little further, if you suspect that your swing plane is too upright or flat, just have a friend post himself to your right so that he can look at you with the target in the distance. If your hands swing up to a point between the right shoulder and the neck, then you are too upright. If your hands swing up to a point outside or to the left of the right shoulder as he views it, then your swing has gotten too flat. Of course, if your hands swing up to point over the tip of your right shoulder, cease worrying. You're in fine shape.

Another point. Provided you don't let go of the club with your hands, bend your left arm more than a tad, or collapse the right leg, how far you swing back is simply a product of your build. Jack Nicklaus swings past the horizontal position with woods and long irons at the top; so does Gary Player. And if you need a further example, take me! I swing way past horizontal, but I'm tall and flexible. Even so, there is really no absolute as to how far you swing back.

Actually, there is a trend today toward longer backswings. And I, for one, am all for it. Because I think the shorter backswing in vogue a few years ago was actually the product of the "keep the left heel down, restrict the turning of the hips" school, and you know what I think about that. Take any of the great players, Snead, Nicklaus, Weiskopf, and Player, and they swing the club and they swing it full.

Having said all this about the position at the top, I should really point out that in fact there is no such position. It's simply a technical term that everybody—pros and amateurs alike—has gotten used to. It's a convenience, as it were, for study.

For the phrase "top of the backswing" we should really be talking about the change in motion from backswing to downswing. I think you should definitely be conscious of this change in motion, as it's where most of the problems occur in the golf swing after your address position.

Many, many golfers appear to take the club back well, but, when they try to change the motion of the club from the backswing to the downswing, something breaks down. To me this breakdown has a lot to do with tempo.

If you take the club back slowly, the change in motion is a lot easier, I have found. And here I want to interject something that has really been dynamite for me and has helped a lot of amateurs I've told it to.

It's this. If a golfer has too fast a backswing, and wants to slow it down to the right pace, then it's no good simply telling him to take it back slowly—he can't do that. The only way to correct a fast backswing is to tell him to take the club out of the bag slowly, walk to the ball slowly, tee the ball up slowly, spread his feet slowly, waggle slowly, forward press slowly. Then, and only then, will he take it back slowly.

The reason why people get too fast going back is they say to themselves, "Gee, everybody's watching, I've got to tee it up quickly, hit it quickly." You have 'to quit that. Don't rush around. Even looking at your target before the stroke, making decisions on the type of shot you want and the club you want to hit, don't rush. Don't, of course, take eight hours to hit, but, when it's your turn to play go through your preshot routine at a nice, even tempo.

I would say at least 50 per cent, possibly more, of good tempo is developed before you ever get over the ball. If you don't believe me, watch Snead, watch Nicklaus, watch Boros. And if you're from the old country, you may still get a chance to watch Bobby Locke. Watch them and see how they do everything methodically. You'll soon agree that slow backswings go along with slow actions before the swing.

Another way to control the pace of your swing is an image I use relating the speed of your swing to the revolutions per minute (RPM) of a car engine. (See color section, illustration 13.) For the sake of argument, suppose your swing has a red line at 7,000 RPM but you are able to go up to 7,500 RPM without blowing up the engine. Now your best function is at 7,000 RPM, the place where you get the most power. But so many people don't know what their red line is in golf. It's as though they were driving a high-powered sports car without a tachometer.

Now there isn't any rev counter available for the golf swing, but I can tell you how to find out your personal red line. Go out to the practice ground one time and, after warming up, try to swing as hard as you can, noting the distance you get. On each succeeding swing ease back a little until you find you lose distance. Just above that point, where you lose distance, is your personal red line. It's the speed of swing that delivers optimum power for you with no risk of "blowing" the engine of your swing.

Certainly I know the pros out on tour have learned this lesson well. I went down to the first Tournament Players' Division driving contest in Atlanta and Lee Trevino got up on the tee, and I thought to myself, "Boy, he's really going to be able to hit it." He swung as hard as he could, but he looked exactly as if he was swinging normally! And this was true of every pro who entered the contest. I expected to see some big, different "flail" actions and yet, while all of them swung as hard as they could, their swings looked like their regular swings, exactly. You would think they'd get up and make the biggest motion you've ever seen and beat the ball to death.

Even Jack Nicklaus was the same. Jack hit it as hard as he could, but I defy anyone to tell his long-drive swing from his regular swing.

In other words, *all* of us pros are swinging very close to our maximums all the time. And yet to the onlookers I bet that it didn't seem the boys were making *that* much effort. The moral of this is obvious: You can make such a big old fast swing that it actually gets you less distance than one at a slightly slower tempo. How much slower your red line is from your top RPM possible I can't tell you. You'll just have to throttle back from the maximum yourself some time and find out. But I know that you'll be a far better golfer if you take the trouble to do just that. You'll find when you swing a little under your maximum you'll hit it just as far and much more solidly.

Besides advocating a slow backswing, I would recommend if possible a pause at the top. This, I find, enables me to get everything together up there; makes me feel the position of my hands, and then I can just pull on through.

I've really worked on that pause. When I was still an amateur, I used to go out on the practice tee and just hold the club at the top for a second or two, and then just pull on through. Ever since then, I've had a little pause at the top.

Today, I probably have less of a pause than I did a couple of years ago, but I can honestly say that I've never had any trouble in any tough situation in a tournament with tempo breaking down. Some people get quicker, some people get flippy, but because of my methods—slow back, pause at the top, and then pull through—I've never had a problem with tempo.

In baseball, a pitcher can throw a ball with maximum force only by shifting his weight from one side to the other. It's the same principle in golf.

The early set of the wrists helps me to feel where the club and clubface are throughout the backswing. It eliminates a lot of movement at the top of the swing and allows a later release in the downswing.

In comparison to Jack Nicklaus, who makes wider extension of the club so that his wrists break late in the swing because of the early set, my wrists are almost fully cocked at the halfway point.

Hinging the right arm correctly is important for both positioning and swing plane. At the top of the swing the right arm should hinge to allow the shaft of the club to point over the tip of the right shoulder directly at the target.

I've talked at some length now about the pause at the top, but I should explain how it works. It's really more of a mental image, or "feel" thing, in a way, than a fact. But it's nonetheless important.

You have to understand that the various parts of the body do not complete their backswings at the same time. They wind up sequentially. The knees and hips will complete their backswing before the shoulders, the shoulders will complete their backswing before the arms, and while most of the wrist cock is done early in the backswing, there is a tad more wrist cock at the top. This additional wrist cock occurs due to the pull of the clubhead on the hands as the club finishes its backswing, and also because of the pull of the left side which initiates the downswing. The shaft bending in response to the change of direction causes the wrists to achieve their "maximum" cocked position.

In fact, the left leg makes its move into the downswing just as the hands and club have completed their backswing. Then there is a time lag before the pull initiated by the left leg travels up the left side and is felt in the hands. This time lag is the pause you feel. But it is a vital feel to have because it's proof to you that your change of direction is correct.

You begin the downswing in the same way that you started the backswing, by a move from the knees. To be more precise, the knees move laterally toward the target. The reasoning is the same as on the backswing, too. On the backswing, you had to shift your weight to the right foot. As you start down, your weight is still on your right foot, and, as has been said, you must have your weight on the left foot in the downswing. So the knees go to work. The left knee pulls to the left and the right knee drives right behind it with a push off the right foot.

I want you to be quite certain on this point. It's the knees that start the downswing, not the hips. So many teachers, and well known ones, too, still insist on a "lateral shift of the hips" initiating the downswing. This is a bunch of bunk. In reality, you can't turn your hips without the legs initiating the movement.

If you ever move your hips laterally this will in turn force your head to move laterally, too. Then your whole upper body will get in front of the ball by impact, and you will be trying to do the impossible—hit a ball that is *behind* you.

The reason why people think that there is a lot of lateral movement in the hips is because the knee action is so prominent. At the top of the swing, the left knee has moved so far right as you look at him that when the left knee moves back in the first move of the downswing to return the weight to the left foot, it has made a large lateral movement. But the lateral movement is predominantly in the knees, not the hips.

At the World Series, I stood there with Jack Nicklaus and Tom Weiskopf and I wasn't even worried about what I was doing—I was trying to figure out this point in the swing. So I held up my driver to see whether they moved their hips toward the target from the address position, and, if it was more than an inch or two, I'll go take an eye test! There was *no* lateral movement of the hips for all practical purposes. It was the knees that moved. After the legs initiate, everything from the navel down drives and turns, which causes the upper body to ride in their wake.

Now the next point on the legs in the downswing is that, in the same way that you set your right leg solid in the backswing and coiled against it, so in the downswing you have to have something to hit against. That something is your left leg. You have to set your weight on your left foot and set the left leg solid; your hip, knee, and foot should be braced.

Here's how you do it. You may remember that I talked about Percy Boomer's image for the hips in the backswing. But that, you know, is a great image for the downswing, too. Here again, your knees must not bend or straighten any more than they did at address because otherwise your hips would drop or raise and the whole body would drop or raise and the radius of your swing would shrink or expand. If either happens, you'll have a lot of mishits.

Now if you drive your knees toward the target, then your hips will turn as though they were in that barrel. The hips turn to the left, out of the way, and the left leg will eventually turn out of the way into a solid position to resist the hit.

The action of the knees triggers a chain reaction in the upper body. The lateral motion of the left knee acts and pulls on the left hip, as we've seen. The turn of the hips out of the way then initiates a release of the coiled muscles in the left side of the back and starts the pulling action in the left side and arm down toward the ball. This pulling action with the left arm is very much akin to a back-handed stroke in tennis for a southpaw—the only difference is that the plane of the stroke is the golf plane, not a tennis plane, which is more horizontal.

The left-sided pulling action brings the upper body—trunk, shoulders, arms, wrists, and club—down in one piece. In other words, they are doing nothing at this point except allowing themselves to be pulled down by the left side. They retain the same shape they were in at the top of the swing. In other words, the wrists stay cocked, and the right arm is still bent in the same "ready" position.

The head, and especially the shoulders, also retains the same position, and this is worth a few words by itself.

The head must not be allowed to drift forward in the downswing. Otherwise, the body gets ahead of the ball and you lose power. Since the head is where we feel that we as individuals are, a good image to have is to feel that you (your head) are staying behind the ball as you uncoil in the downswing. This gives you a steady platform to hit off.

And here I would like to digress a little to take care of a couple of mistaken ideas about the downswing. First, a lot of people say that the downswing is all left-sided and that the right side does nothing or is passive, or words to either effect. Bunk! It's a two-sided game, for the umpteenth time. Your right arm is your whole lever system. You can't hit the ball anywhere just using the left arm. Your right arm has most of the power.

Let me explain. You start the swing with a pretty straight right arm. You swing back and the right arm and the right wrist hinge. Now all you do to bring the club back to square at impact is release the hinge in the elbow, which in turn releases the right wrist and returns the clubhead to square. But the problem is that a lot of people get to the top, create the hinge correctly in the right arm and wrist, and then release too early. As a result, the player loses power and the clubhead, depending on how the body is positioned in the hitting area, returns to anything but a square position.

But the real importance of the unhinging action is that, in co-operation with the backhanded hit in the left hand, it creates the power in the swing. It's the unhinging of the right elbow that triggers the release of power from right arm to right wrist to club. It's the same in almost every sport.

I call this action the "release of the angles," the release of the angles you created in the right arm and wrist at the top of the swing.

And here's the other misconception. The power in the downswing does not come from the legs alone. To hear a lot of people talk, you would think that the legs were everything. Not so.

When you throw a rock into the water, the ripples move outward in successive waves. The ideal downswing is the same thing. The first ripple is the legs, and the rest of the body follows at logical intervals after it in the order we've described.

Leg action is important in that, the faster and more positively you can move your legs, the more power you are going to generate. If your legs are slow, you will have to be overactive with your shoulders, arm, and hands. But the whole downswing has to be a co-ordinated action. And the most powerful action of them all is the "release of the angles."

The release of the angles is also responsible for good club speed. No, I haven't made a mistake; I did not mean clubhead speed.

I think that many golfers make the mistake of swinging the clubhead and not the whole club. But what gets you the big distance is *club* speed. The really long straight hitters get the speed right in the middle of the shaft. The whole club is really moving.

Whereas many wild hitters have the clubhead going 125 miles an hour and the top of the club is doing almost nothing.

So when I am approaching impact, I'm giving it a two-sided effort. The left side is pulling and I'm releasing the angle in the right arm, but my intent is to allow both sides to really move the whole club on and through into the finish. The angles in the right arm never fully release until after impact. That way, you get real distance.

I can actually feel impact. I feel that I'm returning the back of the left hand and the palm of the right hand to the imaginary "wall" I created at address. The reason I can feel impact, I am convinced, is that I use a square grip. If your grip is not square, either too strong or too weak, it's tough to feel impact, as your hands are, so to speak, off center.

Another good idea at impact is one I picked up from Lee Trevino, who is full of original ideas on the golf swing. He places an imaginary line running from the ball up the middle of your body. Then at impact he tries to drive his right knee past the line. Lee's idea is of particular value if you suspect that your right leg is not driving hard enough in the downswing.

While we're talking about Lee, you may remember my talking about his strong grip and the closed clubface position that results at the top of the backswing. At impact, a golfer with Lee's type of action has to make a blocking move—keep the hands well ahead of the clubhead—to prevent the face from closing. This is solely because of his grip. Whereas a player using a square grip, as I recommend, can release naturally—allow the hands to turn over soon after contact has been made. The hands will be only slightly ahead of the ball at impact as they were at address. This advanced hand position of Lee's also accounts for the lower flight of his shots. The farther ahead the hands are, the more loft is taken off the club and the lower the ball will fly.

There's so much clubhead speed for the first two or three feet of the follow-through that the follow-through is really just a by-product of what you've done before. But the follow-through does repay study, as it shows whether you made a good swing before. You're never going to have a pretty follow-through unless you have a pretty downswing and impact.

The pulling from the left side and the release of angles in the right arm send the club flying through the ball. A couple of feet after impact the right arm straightens out, and that, funnily enough, is the only place where both arms are perfectly straight. The arms almost seem to fly on their own until the club points straight at the hole in what is called the "extension" position. I believe in a long extension through the ball. If you don't achieve this position in the follow-through, then it means that one side of the body or the other is not doing its work.

However, I don't believe in fighting the folding action of the left arm that takes place soon after both arms are fully extended. In the backswing the right arm folds to create the lever and your left arm remains straight. In the follow-through, your right arm extends and your left arm must fold to create your greatest clubhead speed because you're getting your greatest freedom of movement.

If your left arm never broke down, you'd break a bone. Arnold Palmer does that. He fights that breaking down of the left arm, which is not a natural movement. If he weren't so strong, he'd have no chance.

In the finish, your hips and shoulders should all be looking right at the target. Not past the target or before the target, but right on it. The tilt of the body should be according to your plane. If you have a flat plane to your swing, you will be standing more upright, your hands high, with the shoulders level like Hogan or Lee Trevino. If you have a more upright swing like mine, then your left shoulder is going to be a little higher than the right.

Another point on the follow-through that Hogan stresses, and I think it's right, is that there is really no tension at the end of the follow-through. You create all the tension going back, and create all the power in the hit, but when your hands finish up over your shoulders you should be relaxed. You shouldn't have a feeling of power, or of tension. You should just have the feeling of perfect balance and relaxation. In the backswing, you plant your right leg and let your left side go by it. And in the downswing, you plant your left leg and let your right side go by it. So, at the end of the swing, you're balanced easily on the left foot with your body facing the target and your hands and arms relaxed and easy.

Talking about balance and a pretty follow-through reminds me that personally I think Al Geiberger has got the best swing I've ever seen. I've never seen a swing that was better balanced. Weiskopf, Nicklaus, they have good-looking follow-throughs, or even myself or Buddy Allin. But personally, I think that Al has the best-looking follow-through I have ever seen. Watch Al sometime—you'll get a great lesson on perfect balance in motion. And that is tough—staying balanced—for a tall man like Al. I know. I'm tall myself and occasionally I've been known to finish off balance. When I do, remembering Al Geiberger's fine swing helps me visualize the right action and puts me right.

THE FIVE BASIC MOVES

1. *The One-Piece Take-away*

The importance of the moving everything away together in the take-away is that it gets the whole left side into action so that it will swing by the firmly planted right leg. Since you established the position of the right leg at address, you don't have to think about it during the swing.

2. *The Early Set*

The early cocking action sets up the late release. But equally important is the fact that the wrists have to cock *somewhere* and, when they do, they must cock without disturbing the angle in the left wrist. Otherwise, the clubface will not be maintained in a square position. It is not only more natural to set the hands early, it is frankly far easier to do than the late cocking since the club is still in front of you in the early set and the club is traveling so much slower

The Five Basic Moves

1
One-piece
take-away

2
Early set

3
Hinging of
the right arm

4
Knees
start the
downswing

5
Release of
the angles
in the
right
arm

at this early stage of the backswing than toward the end of the back-swing.

3. *The Hinging of the Right Arm and Wrist*

Winding up the right arm and wrist is essential in just about all athletic actions, and golf is no exception. The setting of the right hand so that the shaft points over the tip of the right shoulder, however, is also vital, as it ensures that you're swinging in the right plane.

4. *Knees into the Downswing*

Working on the knees as the first move in the downswing accomplishes many things. The pull of the left knee toward the target transfers the weight to the left foot and establishes a firmly planted left leg. It initiates the clearing action of the hips to the left. It also starts the uncoiling of the left side, initiating the pulling action from the left side and arm and continuing into the backhand hit with the left hand. It also pulls the right and the still cocked right arm down into the hitting area, where the release in the angles in the right arm and wrist will take place. The drive of the right knee adds considerably to power and is an added force to the clearing action of the left side.

5. *The Release of the Angles*

There's no doubt in my mind that the right hand and arm have to hit and hit hard. I'm firmly convinced, too, that there are more problems caused by inactive right arms and wrists or right arms and wrists where the angles are never released than practically anything else in the golf swing. The only provision is that the left side has to pull down first—then you can release the angles as hard as you like.

When I work on my own golf swing, these are the basic moves that I work on. And here I would like to make another point. It's no good working on these moves out of order, whether or not you are simply practicing, and especially if you are trying to locate a problem.

73

The golf swing is a sequential affair; one thing always leads to another. So it's no good working on your take-away if your address position is wrong. It's no good working on setting the angles if your take-away or early set is bad. But work on it in order from the address, through the systematic setup to the five basic moves, and you'll build and build.

ON THE PRACTICE TEE AND OUT ON THE COURSE

The time to work on your swing is in practice sessions. You must never be in the position where you are trying to build your swing on the golf course or in pregame warm-ups.

I know that sounds obvious, but believe me, playing in pro-ams, as I do, I see it all the time. Amateurs just don't seem to understand that there are certain rules on working with the swing that you can violate only at your peril.

Practice sessions should be special times that you set apart for improving your swing or other skills. You shouldn't practice when you're tired, and don't practice past the point where you feel tired. In both cases, your practice sessions will be fruitless. Each practice session should have a specific objective. When you've succeeded in reaching that objective, quit while you're ahead. You then have a foundation on which to build another day. Take it one day at a time. You can't do everything in one session.

If you're trying to make a conscious change in your swing, as opposed to refreshing your mind about ingrained fundamentals, then it's especially important to work on one point at a time. Pick the one that's earliest in the sequence of the swing and get that right first. If you try for two at one time, all you'll do is blow your mind—and whatever swing you have at the time.

Warm-up sessions before a round are just that, warm-up sessions. What you're trying to do is find out what sort of swing you have today. When you find out, accept the fact that you're going to have to live with it. Any attempt to "find a swing on the practice ground" is doomed to failure. It's like last minute boning up before an examination—it tends to push out the material that you learned earlier, in this case your fundamentals. Also, many times I find that I hit the ball only fair in practice, yet super on the course. So don't worry too much about results when warming up. You could well be in for a pleasant surprise later.

Out on the course I never think of my swing except, as you'll see in Chapter 10, that I visualize the type of swing I want to put on the ball. But I accept the fact that others are less skilled than I. So let's discuss what swing keys you can carry out on the course, and how you should use them.

First, don't make a Chinese menu out of it. Don't pick one idea from Column A and another from Column B. Any more than one swing key is fatal.

Second, I think you either have to pick the one thing that is giving you trouble—say releasing the angles—or, even better, use an over-all key that will key the whole swing.

A good example of an over-all swing key is "Swing the whole club, not the clubhead." That's one of my favorites. Or another one I like is "Swing the club like a pendulum." If you're swinging off plane, "Swing from chin to chin"—in the backswing, swing until your left shoulder hits the chin, and through until your right shoulder hits the chin. If you're inaccurate, then "thinking impact at address" is good. Really set the blade and your body square at address and try to feel impact, a square impact, through your address position.

The reason I like an over-all swing key is that out on the course it is too late, really, to work on individual portions of the swing. You run the risk of the swing collapsing on you. But an over-all swing key can get you around on those off days.

The best way to use swing keys is to visualize yourself doing them when you're visualizing the type of the swing you want to make. You must on no account think of them during the swing. However, if you're really desperate, you could take a practice swing while thinking of the particular key, but again never think of it during the swing. Out on the course, you must let the swing happen, for good or ill.

I'll be going into this business of visualizing the swing and the whole matter of programming yourself for a particular shot later in the book. So I won't belabor this point now. However, before I close this chapter on the swing, I must explode just one more myth.

My playing partners in pro-ams come up to me sometimes and ask, "What's the difference between your swing for a four-wood and that for a 2-iron?" They're firmly convinced, you see, that you put a different swing on every club in the bag.

But in reality, I just make the same swing with every club in my bag. As the clubs get longer, my swing has a tendency to get *slightly* longer. But that is much more a product of a slightly faster tempo—as I put a little more effort into it—than the difference in clubs. My 9-iron swing is darned near parallel and my driver is perhaps a little past parallel.

But the main point is you don't consciously swing longer on your driver than your 9-iron or shorter on your 9-iron than your driver. YOU SWING THEM ALL EXACTLY THE SAME.

CHAPTER SIX

Shotmaking, Spins and Other Stuff

Most amateurs have the idea that top players make "secret" swing changes to maneuver the ball. Speaking for myself, I say that's not true. As you'll see, the majority of any changes I make are made *before* I draw the club back, that is, at address. But there is a secret of sorts to shotmaking, and it is that any variation is simply a *slight* modification of the regular straight ball. So logically you have to have a reasonably consistent swing for the modifications to have the desired effect.

It's the same as when you learn to play pool. You first learn to become a pretty good "plain ball" hitter and groove your stroke before going on to putting English or various sorts of spin on the ball. It's essential that you understand this principle. Otherwise, I am going to have chronic slicers, for example, setting up as I advise to hook the ball and, instead, they'll pull the ball straight left.

In short, in this chapter I will assume that you've done your homework on the swing to the point that you can hit the ball reasonably straight. Not that there won't be a lot of information in this chapter that any golfer can use. There will be. Besides covering such advanced shots as curving the ball to the left and right, I'm also going to discuss hitting it high and low, punching the ball and hitting "floaters," as well as the various types of lies you'll encounter in the course of a round.

Curve Balls

Ben Hogan, whom I've studied, was such a masterful player that he could move the ball a dozen different ways without ever changing his grip or changing the plane of his swing. Most club golfers, however, think that, to play an intentional fade, slice, draw, or hook, you have to change your grip and your swing plane. On one hole they'll weaken their grip and swing outside-in to slice it, and the next they'll adopt a strong grip and swing very much inside-out to hook it. Before you know it, they've become totally confused. They lose their normal swing and are in more trouble because of these changes than if they had hit a plain straight ball out of trouble and accepted the loss of distance this entailed.

Not that I'm trying to discourage you from learning these shots —far from it. They will really save you strokes once you've mastered them. Let me give you an example.

I was playing the seventeenth hole in the last round of the 1975 Atlanta Classic, and frankly I hadn't been playing well. But if I could par in I would make a nice check. On this tight, heavily wooded par-4, I left my drive to the right and it wound up behind a tree in the right rough which was directly in my path to the pin. My options were either to chip out sideways and then face a full medium iron into the green, or attempt to slice the ball around the

78

tree and get it up near the green. The best I would have made probably from chipping out was a 5, allowing for the short iron and two putts. But the slice shot offered me a much better chance at a 4. Even if I missed the green, the worst I would face was a bunker shot, and I'm a good bunker player, or a short chip or pitch shot. So I sliced a long iron out of there, and it flew into the bunker, on the left of the green; I wedged out and holed the putt for 4.

But you see what I mean. Learning these curve ball shots doesn't make it a lead pipe cinch that you'll recover and make par, but these shots will advance the ball closer to the green, and that's the name of the game—the closer you can get to the green with the shot at hand, the better your chances of scoring well on the hole.

CURVES TO THE RIGHT

A ball that curves to the right is the result of the clubface being open in relation to the swing line, the path the clubhead follows through impact. The clubhead cuts across the ball, making it travel across the clubface from the center toward the toe and imparting a left-to-right spin.

However, you may remember that I said earlier that I always place the clubhead behind the ball so that it is square to the target. How is it possible for the clubhead to be in this square position at impact and yet cause the ball to spin to the right? The answer is: by alignment of the body and therefore the swing line through the ball to the left of the target. The line of the swing will always follow the direction in which your feet, hips, and shoulders are aligned.

So, if you set up with your whole address position aligned at an imaginary target to the left, and have the leading edge of the club set squarely at the target, the clubface is open in relation to the line of swing and produces a ball that starts left of target and then swings back left to right to the target.

Here I want to clear up a misconception about a fade, a ball that curves only slightly from left to right, and a slice, a ball that

79

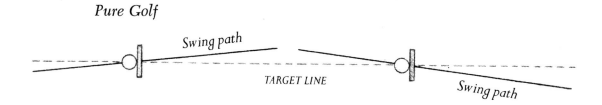

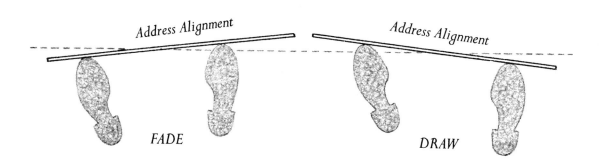

Minor changes to the address position enable you to curve the ball to the right or left without making major changes to the swing itself. For example, to play a fade, simply align at a secondary target to the left, and set the clubface square to your real target. Since the swing line will parallel your feet, the clubface will return to the ball moving across the target line with the face in a slightly open position and impart the necessary left-to-right spin. The opposite is true for a draw. Align to the right with the clubface square, then swing normally. The clubface will be returned to a slightly closed position and the ball will draw.

curves really viciously from left to right. There's no essential difference between deliberately producing either of them. They're the same family of shot. The only difference is the degree to which you align your body and feet to the left of target.

For example, when I won the Phoenix Open in '74, coming up to play my second shot at the seventeenth hole, I heard a roar from the gallery on eighteen as Lanny Wadkins' putt dropped for an eagle 3. This meant I had to finish par-birdie or vice versa to tie him.

It is important to understand the over-all swing speed that works best for you. Like driving a sports car, you must know where the red line is, the place where you get the most power.

Club speed is achieved by creating angles in the right arm and wrist in the backswing, then releasing them in the downswing. At the top of the swing, the arm and wrist are fully cocked. At the halfway point of the downswing,

they remain cocked. Then the release begins, creating maximum speed through the hitting area.

The downswing is initiated with a lateral move of the knees. As the left knee pulls, so the right drives behind it. The hips then start to turn out of the way. However, there must be almost no lateral movement in the hips, otherwise your upper body will get ahead of the ball.

At that point, I was, as we say on tour, "in between clubs." I couldn't decide whether to go with a 5- or 6-iron. It was exactly 165 yards to the pin. My 6-iron travels 160 and my 5-iron 170. Because the pin was tucked over on the right side of the green I felt a faded 5- would work best for me. The shot came off as planned. It started twenty feet left of the pin, faded back, hit and spun right, coming to an abrupt halt not six inches from the hole. This charged me up and I went on to birdie the last hole and win.

Now on this shot at Phoenix, I aimed around thirty feet left of the pin initially. But on that slice shot around the trees I described earlier in this chapter, I had to aim off more like thirty yards. But they were both the same type of shot, the only difference being the degree I aligned my body and feet left of the hole at the address. You can see then that the plane is always the same. It's just how much the face is open that dictates the amount of curve.

You may have noticed that on the Phoenix Open shot I said I aligned myself thirty feet left of the pin, but the ball started out only twenty feet left of the pin. Well, most players don't realize that, when you hit a fade or slice, the ball, with the face open, will always start to the right of the direction in which you're swinging through impact. Because the club is open, the ball has a tendency, at the point of impact, to slide toward the toe. When aligning yourself to play a slice-spin shot, you must take this push factor into consideration. Lee Trevino is the perfect example of a tour player who plays a push fade.

Another point can be best illustrated by an example. A golfer plans to fade or slice, aligns himself correctly to the left of the target, and hits—straight ball to the left! What happened? He released his right hand too soon, it closed the clubface to a position where it was square with the line on which he was swinging, and so it went straight left.

There's an easy way to guard against this happening to you. All you do is increase the pressure in the left hand a little and decrease the pressure in the right. You do this as you set up on the shot. As an added precaution, feel that you are delaying the release in the an-

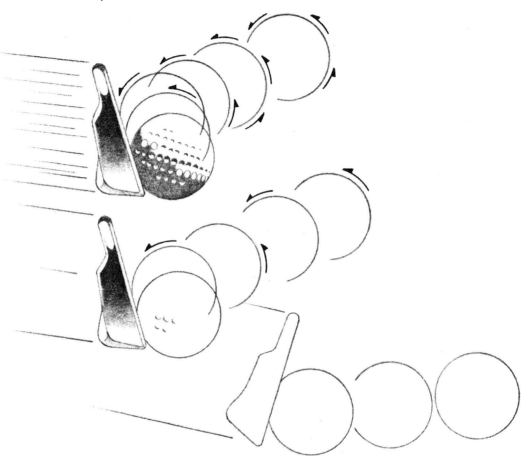

As an added precaution to ensure that the ball curves in the right direction, I either increase or decrease the amount my left hand leads the clubhead through the hitting area. For a fade, I'll delay the release (left) by increased pressure in my left-hand grip at address. For a right

gles of the right arm and right wrist. This way your left hand will lead into the shot, the clubface will stay open through impact, and the shot will come off as planned. In fact, the more slice-spin you want to put on the ball, the more you have to lead with the left hand through impact.

Two final points about the fade/slice shots, both relating to club selection. First, don't expect to move the ball in the air from left

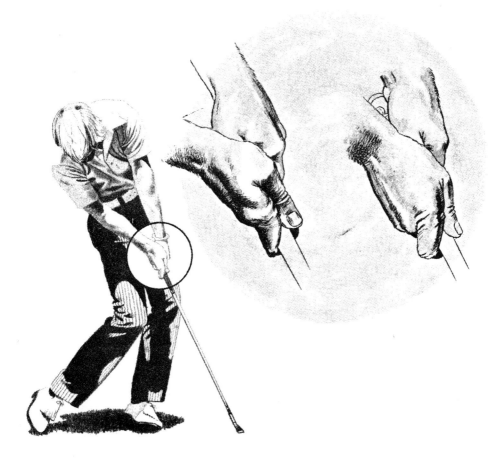

draw, I'll increase the pressure in my right hand at address so that I get an earlier release; my right hand rolls over the left quicker, and the clubface closes (right).

to right much with anything more lofted than a 7-iron. The reason is that on the short irons the backspin you get is greater than any side-spin you can apply. That's why most high-handicappers love short irons—they can't slice them! So, if you want to bend the ball to the right, the club to select is anything from a 2- to a 7-iron. Second, you have to realize that a faded shot won't go as far as a straight shot with the same club. So, you have to go to a club one, two, or even three numbers stronger than usual depending on whether you're hitting a fade, a moderate slice, or an enormous slice.

CURVES TO THE LEFT

As you would expect, the reason a ball curves to the left is exactly the opposite of that for the fade/slice balls. To draw (slight curve to left) or hook (extreme curve to left) the ball, the clubface must be closed in relation to the line of swing. This imparts a right-to-left spin to the ball.

The technique for playing drawn or hooked shots is also the opposite of that for fades and slices. You align your body and feet to the right of target and then close the blade so that the leading edge of the blade is aimed right at the pin. Thus, at impact, the clubface is closed in relation to the line of swing producing the draw or hook. And again, the degree of curve produced is in direct relation to the amount you align yourself to the right of target. A slight alignment to the right produces a draw, a more drastic alignment to the right, a hook.

The flight characteristics of the draw/hook family are also opposite to the fade/slice shots. Remember that for the left-to-right shots the clubface was open. But the closed face used on the draw/hook shots traps the ball on the face so that the ball flies initially directly along the direction of the swing, then it curves left.

This characteristic of drawn and hooked shots makes them easy to play through an opening in trees. You simply aim your stance at the opening and the clubface at the pin, knowing the ball will fly straight through the opening before it curves to the left. The same can't be said for faded or sliced shots—you're simply going to have to practice these to the point where you know how far right of your swing line they are going to fly at the start.

In the same way that allowing the face to close at impact was disastrous on a deliberate fade or slice, so allowing the face to stay open through impact on a planned draw or hook will completely wreck the shot. Another way of saying it is that, if you block out a deliberate draw or hook, you can get a shot flying straight to the right. The way you prevent it is to relax your left-hand grip a little and firm up the grip of the right hand. This will encourage a slightly earlier release of the angles in the right arm than normal.

In selecting the right club to draw or hook the ball, watch the following points. By closing the face, you're taking loft off the club. So first of all, make certain that the club you've selected has enough loft on it after you've closed the face to get the ball in the air. The other consideration is that a drawn or hooked shot will always go farther than a straight shot with the same club, because you're reducing the loft by closing the clubface. So go to a weaker club than normal if you're planning to bend the ball to the left. The only exception to this is a snap hook—that type of shot comes back to the ground so fast it won't give you as much distance as usual unless the ground is hard.

In concluding this section on curve balls, I want to make some general points that apply whichever way you're trying to move the ball. First, don't depart from your regular swing tempo in playing these shots. If you do you may very well accentuate the spin on the ball and so magnify the resulting curve more than planned. Second, I don't want any golfer to use the instructions I have given here to correct a faulty swing. If you're a chronic slicer, for example, closing the blade will only be a temporary cure at best, and in the long run it will only compound your problem. Two wrongs—such as an outside-in swing and closed blade—do not make a right. Until you get your swing square and are returning the clubface to the ball along the target line, you had better forget about maneuvering the ball. These instructions will work only if you hit the ball straight—your swing is on a plane—or at most with a slight fade or draw. Chronic slicers and hookers, again, forget it!

One thing we haven't covered so far is how the lie of the ball affects your ability to hook or slice the ball. As a general rule, when the ball is sitting down on a close lie, your general tendency will be to cut or fade the ball. The reason for this is that, to get the ball up,

Before swinging, I visualize in my mind the shot I'm about to play. If it's a straight shot I want, I'll picture my own swing. For a fade, I see

Lee Trevino's swing. And for a draw, I visualize the late Tony Lema's swing. Then I just carry the image into the shot.

you will tend to make a longer lead with the left hand through the ball, which will leave the clubface open at impact. The opposite is true when the ball is sitting up high in the grass or, for that matter, when it is teed up. You'll then tend to hook it, because you can release the hands a little more.

Lastly, I can't impress on you enough the importance of visualizing the type of swing and the desired trajectory of the shot before you address the ball. I have three "visual swings" in my bag; when I want to hook it, I just think of Tony Lema's old swing; when I want to fade it, I think of Lee Trevino's swing, and when I want to hit it straight, I just visualize my own swing. I can honestly say that I've never in my life hooked a ball I've tried to fade, or vice versa, and one good reason for it is visualizing the type of swing I need in advance of the shot.

HITTING IT HIGH AND LOW

When I was a junior, I had a very instructive lesson from my father. One day he took me out to Harding Park in San Francisco, with a bag of balls and some clubs, and steered me into a small grove of trees. When we were almost in the middle of the grove, he dropped the balls on the ground and pointed to some openings in the tops of the trees, and said, "Hit through those openings."

At first I found it very difficult to select a club that would get the ball that high. Many of the shots crashed against the branches and fell to the ground. But the more shots I hit, the easier it became to judge the right height. And today, when I hit one into the woods, I'm confident that I can find an opening somewhere.

So my first suggestion to you is: Head for the woods. Look for the openings in the top of the trees and spend some time trying to get some balls up and out of there. You'll not only develop accuracy and confidence in your ability to recover, but above all else, you'll learn how to hit the ball high.

In order to hit the ball high, the first move you make is to play

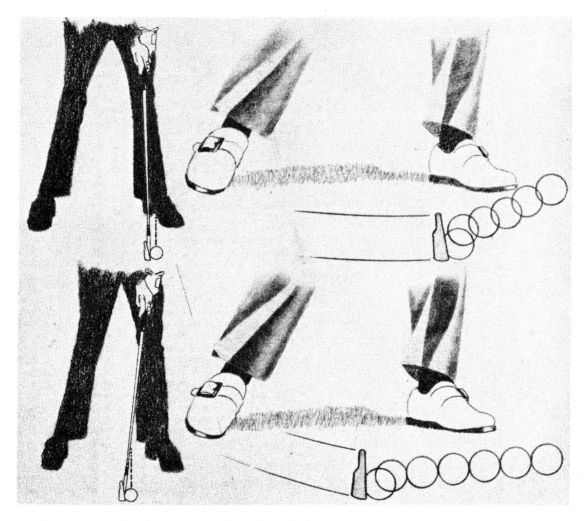

To hit the ball high, simply position the ball farther forward, to the left of your normal ball position, and widen your stance. For a lower shot, move the ball back toward your right foot and narrow your stance.

the ball a little farther forward and widen your stance. I normally position the ball off my left heel. On a high shot, I would position it more off the middle of my left foot. Next, I widen my stance by moving my right foot a few inches to the right. This puts your whole upper body, and especially your head, behind the ball, which is essential to get the ball up quickly. That's about it; ball forward and a slightly wider stance. Leave the rest to your normal swing.

Now if you want to hit the ball really high, then you should release the angles in the right arm and wrist a little earlier. This will give even more additional loft on the club than is provided by moving the ball forward in your stance.

The foregoing assumes that you have a really good lie. If you have the ball sitting in a hole, there's no way these techniques are going to help. In fact, you will either top the shot or hit it fat. If the ball's sitting down, then you'll have to open the blade and cut the ball up in the air. In other words, you use fade/slice techniques I told you about earlier.

To hit the ball low, you reverse the move in ball position you made for hitting the ball high. You moved the ball forward in the stance to hit it high. So, to hit it low, you move the ball position back toward your right foot. The lower you want the ball to go, the farther you move it back in your stance.

So that you appreciate what happens when you move the ball back or forward in your stance, I would like you to take hold of a 7-iron and take your regular stance for the club. First, move the club forward a couple of inches toward the target, keeping the blade square—in other words, the leading edge of the blade is still at right angles to the target line. The hands should stay in the same position as they were originally. See what has happened? You have added loft to the club. That's what you're doing to the blade on a regular high spot. Now return the club to the position on a normal shot. We're now going to go the other way. Start moving the club back toward the right foot, down the target line. Again, keep the leading edge of the blade square to the target line. The farther you move the club to the right, the more you reduce the loft.

Adding or subtracting loft from a club has a direct effect on the club selection. Broadly speaking, if you hit a high shot with a club, it won't go as far as normal. The reverse is true for low shots. However, don't make the mistake of taking a 2-iron because you've got to keep a shot low and then playing the ball opposite your right foot. Do it and you'll see what I mean—you've reduced the loft so much that it's now got reverse loft and the ball will never get up at all! So, you have to really study the effect on the loft you're making by playing the ball back in your stance. Although the same thinking applies to high shots, it's not as critical because you can only advance the ball in your stance a matter of inches forward of your regular ball position, otherwise you won't catch the ball solidly. Whereas you can—and must sometimes—play the ball back in your stance. In other words, you have greater leeway moving the ball right than you do moving it left.

As regards the technique of the low shot, also known as the "knockdown" or "punch shot," you play the ball a little back in your stance as described previously so that the blade is somewhat hooded, that is, the loft is somewhat reduced but the blade is still square to the target. The grip pressure should be equal in both hands and increased slightly to make sure that your swing isn't too wristy. The shot is similar to the controlled fade or slice in that you again want to delay the release of the hands. You use about half your normal follow-through and almost literally point the club at your intended target.

A common mistake on this shot is to sway forward into the shot on the downswing. To prevent this happening, make sure your head and upper body stay behind the ball through the hit.

THE FULL SWING AND THE "FLOATER."

In the old days, Harry Vardon, Francis Ouimet, and the rest of the guys played and won their championships with only seven or eight clubs in their bags. Today, we have fourteen clubs and there's no doubt that has made the game easier.

But don't think for a moment that the modern matched set will totally eliminate the need for "in between" shots. As an example, I am going to run through the distances I get with the various clubs in my bag.

The average distances I get with each club on a full shot are as follows: sand wedge, 95 yards; pitching wedge, 115 yards; 9-iron, 125 yards; 8-iron, 140 yards; 7-iron, 150 yards; 6-iron, 160 yards; 5-iron, 170 yards; 4-iron, 190 yards; 3-iron, 200 yards; 2-iron, 215 yards; 4-wood, 225 yards; 3-wood, 240 yards; driver 280 yards.

You'll notice that my 9-iron is sort of weak at 125 yards, when the 8-iron will hit it at 140 yards. Then there's the big range in my 4-iron—it goes 20 yards farther than the 5-iron. Now that's just my set, but I'm sure that if you study your set you'll find similar gaps between clubs.

How should you play these in-between shots? Well, you may remember that I said earlier that I swing all my clubs to just about the same length. I do, and the reason is, I have found, if you swing short on a club you'll tend to rush the tempo, and very possibly jerk the stroke. I think it's a lot easier to swing each club full and just adjust your tempo when you want less distance.

I've got a lot of precedent on my side in this. Dutch Harrison, who was pro at the Olympic Club in San Francisco when I was in my teens, was famous for his soft shots, and today Sam Snead is still showing us how to play this shot.

I screw up a lot of people when they look in my bag. They see me using this great big swing and they say to themselves, "He must be hitting a full shot." They take the same club and fly the green because they hit each shot full! So the word around the tour is: "Don't watch Miller's bag!"

But soft shots aren't just for those times when you are in between clubs. For example, if you hit an iron into a green that slopes from back to front, and you hit the ball with your flat-out swing, because of the amount of spin resulting from the additional force, you're liable to suck it back to below the hole or even off the front of the green. If there's a water hazard in front of the green, this can haunt you—that's what happened to Ben Hogan at Cherry Hills, and that shot cost him his chance at a fifth U. S. Open victory.

You see, if you hit a shot flat out, you get maximum backspin, but you don't always want maximum backspin. There are times when a shot that lands softly on the green with no spin is ideal.

Take the seventh hole at Pebble Beach. Players take a hard 9-iron into that green, watch it suck back twenty feet below the hole, and say, "How bad a break can you get?" Now if you just choke down on an 8-iron and put a real soft smooth swing on it, the ball will hit right up by the hole and stay.

Very few people try the "soft" shot—maybe because they don't know about it. But all I know is that the shot has won me a lot of money. Whenever I get the right sort of situation, I use it every time.

There's a variation on the plain "soft" shot, and that's called the "floater." In reality, another name for it could be the "supersoft" shot. You take two clubs stronger than you would normally. Hold the club with equal pressure in both hands, but with less pressure than you would use for a normal shot. Now put a full, very slow, lazy swing on the ball. The ball will "float" through the air (hence the name) and when it hits it hardly moves. I should add that on a "soft" shot you would use less grip pressure than normal, but use a little more pressure than on a floater.

ROUGH STUFF

When the average golfer goes into rough, too often he gets up to his ball and the first question he asks himself is, "What club do I need to reach the green?" That is putting the cart before the horse, in my book.

Sure, the distance to the green is one factor, but the first thing to look at is your lie. It's no good fingering a wood when you have a sand wedge lie on your hands. The lie you have in most instances dictates the type of shot you have to hit.

For example, suppose your ball is in a fluffy lie where, if you grounded the club behind the ball, the ball might move on you and cost you a one-stroke penalty. What you have to do is hit the ball as though you were in a fairway bunker. You grip down the shaft an inch or so, depending on how much the ball is elevated above the ground. Hold the clubhead slightly off the ground and stand slightly more erect than usual. The club should rest comfortably in your hands. Now swing smoothly and make a conscious effort to sweep the ball off the grass. Hitting down on a ball that is setting up high is fatal. You might just go right underneath it.

Another point to watch for is whether your ball is up in the grass to some extent or whether it is down on the ground. It makes a considerable difference to how the ball will react.

For example, if I have a 5-iron shot where the ball is sitting just off the ground in two inches of light rough, I know that the ball will travel five yards farther than normal because of the roll factor. A 3-iron from the same lie will not carry the ball as far. However, additional roll makes up for the loss of carry. You get more roll because you can't get the pinching action on the ball you get off the fairway. But if the ball were in the same type of rough but this time sitting on the ground, then you could get a "shooter," or "flyer"—the shot that even the pros are scared of. The ball might go a ridiculous amount farther than normal. If you get that type of lie, then play it conservatively by going to a weaker club so that, if it flies on you, you'll make the green, and if not, then you'll be up in front of the green for an easy chip shot.

Another good reason for going to a weaker club is that from a lie that could produce a "flyer," either the ball will go this ridiculous amount farther than normal—or it will go nowhere. So a more lofted club is also good insurance against leaving the ball in the rough.

While on the subject of "flyers," I should add that you can get them from some fairway lies. If you're lying in clover, then I'll practically guarantee it. There are also some hairy fairways where you'll get semiflyers, where you hit a 7-iron and get an extra twenty yards. Flyers are caused by grass (or clover) getting between the clubface and the ball at impact. It acts as a lubricant between the clubface and the ball and prevents the clubface gripping the ball as it normally would.

In most long rough, you have to recognize that the long irons are useless. The only time I would suggest a wood in rough would be in grass no longer than three inches high, and even so forget the 3-wood. Go to a 4-wood or, even better, a 5-, 6-, or even a 7-wood, if you have one.

I'm very conservative in the rough, if I face a shot that's a 5-iron distance or longer. I'm going to make sure that I don't get in more trouble. Many people just throw away shots by not making certain of getting out of trouble the first time. Every lie in the rough had a different flight potential, so it's a real science.

As regards technique, I make no changes in my swing if the rough is light. In heavy rough, however, I'll move the ball back a couple of inches in my stance so that I get more of a descending blow. I also pick the club up a little quicker going back so I can hit down more sharply and get less grass between the clubface and the ball.

Another point in heavy rough is the tendency for the heel and hosel of the club to get caught up in the grass through impact. This resistance will tend to close the face of the club. To counteract this tendency, set the blade a little open at address—it'll close to a square position at impact all by itself. The deeper the rough, the more you should open the blade.

Finally, don't attempt to put slice or hook spin on the ball out of the rough unless the lie is so good that it's virtually a "fairway" lie or unless the type of lie lends itself to the spin you want to put on the ball. For example, if the ball is lying up on a tuft of grass so that you can hit the back of the ball, then trying for a hook spin shot is okay. Or, if you have a close lie, you could put slice spin on the ball. However, if the lie is such that you can't guarantee putting the blade squarely on the ball with no grass coming between the clubface and ball at impact, you'll have to settle for a straight ball.

Uphill Lies

When your left foot is higher than your right, the main thing to remember is that the path the clubhead travels through the ball must parallel the slope as closely as possible. If the club went through the ball on a true horizontal path like it would from a normal lie, you would drive the ball right into the hill! So the first adjustment is stand with the body as near as possible at right angles to the hill, and the simple way to ensure that that happens is to tilt your shoulders a little so that the left shoulder is higher than normal. Now if you simulate what we've discussed so far, say, by putting your left foot on a thick book, and take your address position with any club, you'll notice that you've increased the loft on the club. It's obvious, therefore, that you will select a less lofted club than usual to get the distance you need from an uphill lie.

These adjustments are fine for a moderately uphill lie, but what if there's a really big slope? Try it a second and you'll find that if you try now to keep your body at right angles to the slope, your weight is so much on your right foot that you're quite certain you would never get through the ball. So now we have to compromise by allowing the body to do the comfortable thing, be a little more vertical. If you will stand up and simulate a big uphill slope by putting your left foot on a chair, you will make the adjustment automatically. You bent the left knee, right?

There's one more important point on uphill lies. Even despite the adjustments, you are going to find it extremely difficult to get through the ball as fully as usual because the weight will tend to stay back on the right foot. Since this will inevitably cut down on the amount of leg action you can get into the downswing, you will find yourself automatically compensating by hitting more with the hands and arms. As a result you will have a tendency to hook the ball. On the longer clubs—say a 4-iron and up—you'll have to aim a little right of target to allow for the hooking flight. Unless you're a slicer, you'll hook everything. The longer the shot the more hook you can expect. On steep hills, you can offset the hook by using the fade technique I advocated earlier.

A mental image that I've used with considerable success is picturing a wall that runs at right angles to the target line from my left shoulder to the ball at address. I then try to return my hands and the clubface "square" to the wall at impact. Since the wall is at perfect right angles to the target, if I accomplish my task my hands and the clubface will also be square at the point of impact.

With my grip I return to impact in much the same position I was in at address. However, Lee Trevino, because of his strong grip, must make a longer lead with his hands—keep them ahead of the clubhead longer—to prevent the clubface from closing and causing the ball to hook. My grip with my left hand only slightly ahead of the ball and the position you see me in at the point of impact I feel are the reasons I hit the ball as straight as I do with my irons.

In the follow-through, the right arm extends while the left arm folds. The head remains *behind* the ball to allow maximum extension and width of arc through to the finish.

If you have a reasonably flat swing plane, then you'll be inclined to finish standing more upright with your shoulders level. With a more upright swing, like mine, the left shoulder will be slightly higher. A good well-balanced finish indicates that a good swing has been made at the ball.

DOWNHILL LIES

When your right foot is higher than your left, we apply the same reasoning we did on uphill lies, and the adjustments of course work out exactly opposite.

On a moderate downhill lie, get your swing parallel to the slope by tilting your shoulders downhill so that your left shoulder is lower than normal. Also move the ball back in your stance. This takes loft *off* the club, so you have to use a more lofted club than normal.

On an extreme downhill lie, you will again have to compromise by bending the uphill leg; this time it's your right leg that bends. On the downswing, you are going to find it very difficult to stop the legs from getting out ahead of the upper body. You are also going to find it difficult to stop the upper body from going down the slope too, to some extent. This means that the body will be somewhat ahead of the hands through the hit. As the hands will be late in squaring up the blade, the clubface will be slightly open at impact, imparting some slice spin to the ball. Compensate by aiming a little left of target.

BALL ABOVE FEET

On sidehill lies, the main problem is not so much what you *want* to do, but what this type of slope *forces* you to do.

Take the most severe ball-above-feet lie you can imagine—a ball up in a tree at chest height. Look what has happened to your swing plane—it's completely flat or horizontal to the ground. If you take this one step farther and actually hold up a 5-iron as though you were going to hit a ball at chest height, you will notice that the loft of the club itself is going to direct the ball to the left of target. The flat swing plane by itself would tend to give you a hooking flight, but you add the way the loft works in this situation, and you can see that it's inevitable that this type of lie gives you a hooking action. And the severer the lie, the more hook flight you're going to get.

When you stand up to a moderate ball-above-feet lie, the first thing you'll notice is that, to address the ball, you'll be standing more upright with a little less flex in the knees than usual and playing the ball farther from your feet. These are just things you would naturally do if left to yourself. But we know that the more upright posture will give us a flatter swing plane, which in turn is going to give us a big hooking action. Now you can't eliminate the flat plane entirely but you can help yourself a bit by choking down on the club a little. This will let you bend more from the waist, giving a more normal posture and swing plane. When you choke down, it cuts down on the size of arc you have, so you'll get less distance out of the club. So it comes down to two things: Choke down on a stronger club than you would normally use, and stand as close as possible to prevent swinging too flat. And, of course, aim to the right of target to allow for the hook.

When you face a severe ball-above-feet situation, you're going to have to choke down even more and use a much stronger club than usual. Why? Because you're going to find it very difficult to make a big turn without losing your balance. The trick here is only to turn as much as you can without losing balance, but such a restricted action is going to cost you power. You can see now why a severe slope may mean selecting two or even three clubs stronger than normal.

Another point on the severe slope is that, despite all your efforts, you are going to get a pretty big hook. Since you can't change your swing plane for obvious reasons, there's only one other place you can compensate, and that is in the clubface position. By addressing the ball with the clubface slightly open, you can count down the amount of hook.

BALL BELOW FEET

The same thinking we applied to the ball-above-feet will also take us through the problem of the lie where the ball is below the feet.

If left to yourself, you would find it natural to bend over very much from the waist in order to reach the ball and play the ball closer to the feet. Again, you can't totally eliminate these tendencies, but you can help yourself a little by gripping down at the end of the grip, which will help you stand slightly more erect. However, you are still going to get a more upright swing plane than normal, and the tendency still will be to slice the ball.

The slicing tendency on ball-below-feet shots means, of course, aligning yourself left of the target at address. It also means that you're going to get less distance off such a lie than off a flat lie. So again you're going to have to go to a stronger club to get the same distance.

On severe lies, you're going to find that your body turn is automatically restricted. This is again going to cost you power and means going to a much stronger club than you normally use for the distance. At address, close the blade slightly to minimize the slicing action.

There are some points I would like to make that apply to all these "hilly" lies. First, only experience will show you how much adjustment you should make. However, if you have not had much experience and haven't practiced them, then a practice swing can be very helpful. I don't normally advocate practice swings, but they can help off tough lies like these. Second, don't expect to get normal distance off these lies. Logically, since your body is to some extent out of position, it makes no sense to hit too hard and run the risk of losing your balance. Shorten your swing to ensure solid contact. Then, swing smoothly with plenty of rhythm, and you'll find the adjustments I suggest will work just fine for you.

Winding up a chapter on shotmaking and lies makes me acutely conscious that I could write volumes on these subjects by themselves. But let me give you a clue as to how to put all the material together.

I've talked about bending the ball, hitting it high and low and so on, and for convenience and clarity I've talked about each shot or lie in isolation. But so often, out on the course, the situation doesn't call for just a plain hook or a plain slice but for a high draw or a punched fade or some other combination.

When you put all these combinations together and multiply them by all the shades of flight between a regular straight ball on the one hand and the extreme curves, different trajectories and tempos on the other, you can readily see how great players have hundreds of different shots in the bag. At last count, I had some 220 variations!

CHAPTER SEVEN

The Short Game

Before any short shot, the first thing to do is check the lie. This tells
me the type of shot I can play. Then I feed into my mental computer
such things as obstacles between the ball and the hole, the break on
the green, the speed of the green, which way the grain runs, and the
putt I would like to leave myself—all the relevant information that
could influence the choice of shot or selection of a target point. Finally, I visualize the length and type of swing that will do the job.
Only then will I take the club in my hand and play the shot. You
should train yourself to go through the same mental routine on
every shot. Believe me, it will really pay off.

Now let's get to the shots you will have to play and their technique. And in the same way as I first explained the basic swing to

you and then the various modifications that produced different shots, let's start with the basic pitch shot and then discuss the variations.

The pitch shot is just a miniature version of the full swing—whether you make a three-quarter, half, or quarter swing. The same elements that go into the full swing—such as one-piece take-away, early set, setting the angles, knees in the downswing, and release of the angles—are all there, but on a smaller scale. As I said earlier, you swing all clubs the same.

I want to emphasize this point because some teachers have said that the wedge shot is a punched shot, that you should stop the club at about waist height. I don't believe that. Never force the club to start or stop. (Yes, you can play a punch shot with a wedge, as we'll see later, but that's a special shot, for special circumstances.) Any time you try to stop a golf swing, it takes energy. So when you try to stop the momentum of the follow-through, there is a risk you'll raise your left shoulder or make some other mistake.

I believe that if you have a seventy-yard pitch, and there's nothing special you need to do with it, you should not make a violent move into the ball. You should simply swing it back at your normal tempo and then accelerate through the ball. My follow-through on a ninety-yarder looks almost like I'm hitting a 2-iron. I don't try to stop the follow-through, I don't punch down on it or hit down on it tremendously. I just let the clubhead do its own thing. And I don't take big, gouging divots. Byron Nelson, I've noticed, takes really thin divots, and I do too. Get that "hitting down" business out of your head. It's not necessary. Swing correctly and you won't "gouge."

The reason a conscious effort to hit down is unnecessary is that you've taken care of that stuff at address. In the same way that you

Undoubtedly the best way for the average golfer to distance with a wedge is by choking up on the club. But for the more advanced player this has become automatic, so he varies the over-all swing tempo from lazy, to smooth, to crisp.

progressively narrowed your stance from the driver down to the full wedge shot, so you gradually narrow your stance as you get closer to the green and have to use shorter and shorter swings. As you bring your right foot closer to the left, this brings your head farther and farther forward. As you move the weight forward, so you automatically create an ever steeper arc and a more descending blow. It's that simple.

For less experienced players, the best way to vary distance with the short irons is to choke down and vary the length of the swing. For the more advanced player, choking down and varying the length of the swing have become automatic, and he fine-tunes the distance needed for each shot by varying his tempo from lazy to smooth to crisp. These various tempos also account for varied flight and spin characteristics.

One thing I do that I know you'll find useful is adopting a fairly open stance on these shorter shots. It does three things, really. First, by aligning a little left, you will be putting a trace of slice spin on the shot, which is just what you need to make the ball stop fast. Second, you don't create as much torque going back on these shorter shots, so opening the stance shortens your backswing naturally and also gives you a little extra torque to help you start down properly. And, third, the open stance gives you better ball-to-target perspective.

Here I would like to interject something on the clubs you should be using for regular pitch shots. I think that the average golfer should standardize pretty much on the pitching wedge for these shots. And I say this even when I know that I and most of the guys on tour use a sand wedge a lot of the time from under a hundred yards. The reason basically is that we can hit the sand wedge much farther than the average golfer. I personally can hit it up to a maximum of ninety-five yards. But I'm certain that most golfers' maximum with the sand iron is fifty yards at best. When they try to use it for longer shots, they release too early, "scoop" the ball and the heavy sole on the club flies under the ball at impact—and the ball goes higher but no farther.

Not that the sand wedge isn't useful to the average golfer for pitch shots. It is. But what I say is this: learn your *comfortable* maximum distance with the club and then use it for pitch shots within its range, where you need a little more height and bite than the pitching wedge will provide.

Just about everything I told you in the shotmaking chapter applies in the short game. For example, there are occasions when you'll need slice-spin and hook-spin shots, the most obvious being those where the pin is tucked up behind a bunker to one side or other of the green. A side-spin shot will allow you to play for the opening in the green and then kick the ball toward the pin on landing. Don't expect to curve the ball in the air with the pitching wedge. The spin will work for you only when the ball hits the ground. Then you're going to need high and low shots, too, and the technique there is the same. The same goes for shots from bad lies and rough, and the things I told you about the hilly lies hold true also.

However, there are a few extra shots you'll need around the green, and we'll deal with those now. You remember the "soft" shot and the "floater." Well, these shots are still very useful in the short game for just less than maximum shots with your wedge, but when you get closer to the green there's another shot I use all the time that's similar to them but just a little bit different, and that's the lob shot.

The lob shot is basically like throwing the ball underhanded. You literally "lob" the ball to the hole without much force and with almost no wrist action.

In your address you open your stance and play the ball forward a little in your stance. You set the blade down behind the ball a little open. You can use a sand wedge for this shot, or a pitching wedge if the lie is tight or if you need a little more distance. Your hands should be in the irregular position over the ball.

Swing the club smoothly and keep the tempo just as smooth going through. Remember: Use your normal swing, but just make it slower. Visualize swinging like Julius Boros. A good image I use on this shot is to visualize that I have a glass balanced on the clubface in the follow-through. This not only keeps your swing smooth; it also prevents you from getting wristy.

When you have to pitch the ball from the rough, you should play the ball back in your stance so that you can pick the club up sharply and produce a more descending blow, which will get the clubface onto the ball with as little grass as possible in between the clubface and the ball. Make sure you get through the ball on this one. If you don't, and instead quit on the shot, you'll dump the ball well short of the hole.

While I think that the shot I have just described is the best "normal" shot from the rough for the average player, there is another type of shot that some of the other pros on tour use. Essentially what you do is hit a standard sand shot out of the rough. You open the clubface and lay the clubhead an inch or two behind the ball. Then you just "splash" it out like a sand shot. You don't attempt to hit directly on the back of the ball. You hit in back of the ball and take grass and ball out together. If you want to try this shot, fine, but I would say use it only when the rough is so heavy that it's virtually impossible to put the clubhead squarely on the ball.

One of the hardest shots in the game is the pitch shot from hardpan. Obviously, you have to use a pitching wedge or sand wedge to get the ball up. You position the ball maybe an inch or so back from your left heel and then concentrate on hitting the ball solid. The descending blow is exactly like that for a regular wedge shot; ball first, and divot after. As insurance, I'll lay the clubface open slightly so that if I do hit the ball a little heavy, then the clubhead will skid through. If you have the clubface square or hooded, then it will stick in the hardpan. Ideally, the best way to play the hardpan shot would be to pick it clean off the dirt. However, you must have a lot of green to work with before you can do that to guard against the possibility of a thin shot.

Before I get into chipping, there's one other type of shot that should be in your bag. It's commonly called the "bump and run." However, I call it the "punched pitch," because, as you'll see, it's much nearer a punch shot than anything else. This is the shot where you hit the ball into a bank and have it bounce up and onto the green.

Knowing how to play the "punched pitch" really saved me at the '74 World Open. On the fifth hole of the final round I hit the ball over the green. I had a downhill lie with a gully between me and the green, which was really fast and sloped away from me. To attempt to carry the ball over the bank of the green with a sand wedge would have been really difficult. So I took an 8-iron, hit the ball right into the bank, it rolled up a foot and a half from the hole, and I made par. I did almost the same thing again at the next hole, knocked it about three feet away and made par. Those two shots really helped in winning the tournament.

In playing the "punched pitch," the most important thing for the average player to do is to make certain he picks the right club so that he at least hits the bank. You are better off hitting the bottom of the bank than flying right over by picking too lofted a club. Anything from a 5- to an 8-iron will do, but anything more than that and you run the risk of going over everything into more trouble. Move the ball back in your stance and hood the clubface. Hooding the clubface is your guarantee that the shot won't go too high. When you hood the club, it traps the ball and doesn't allow it to climb up the face, and builds a solid hit into the shot. Even if you miss the shot, with the face hooded, you'll miss the shot *lower* than intended, and it can still work out fine.

When I said that you should use anything from a 5- to an 8-iron on this shot, I was talking in terms of the average player. A low handicap player, however, can play this shot effectively using even a sand wedge. This is what I did on the eighteenth hole of the 1975 British Open. I was faced with a thirty-yard shot, with a bank in front of me and a tight pin placement. I hooded the face of my sand club, hit the ball into the bank, and it trickled down onto the green and stopped six inches from the hole. If I'd holed it in I would have been in the playoff.

When it comes to chipping, what I do and what I recommend

to you are two quite different things. I use my wedges almost exclusively, because I use different spin shots in my chipping. Therefore, I find it easier to master just a couple of clubs and produce a variety of shots with them.

I remember one time in the Jackie Gleason at Inverrary Golf and Country Club, Lauderhill, Florida, I came to the last hole and hit a bad drive into the rough. The lie was so bad that I had to lay up short of the green. This left me about thirty yards from the pin, which was way left on the green. I had to go over the corner of the green, but there was not enough green near the pin for me to land the ball close and stop it. The break was from left to right. Since I had a good lie, I decided to hit a hook-spin-chip, which would prevent the ball from sliding to the right. It made the ball run right at the hole despite the break and it finished stiff.

Then, if I'm hitting to a downhill pin placement, I obviously don't want the ball rolling too much; I want some check on it. So what I do is use a pitching wedge and open the face a little, which puts some backspin on it. Uphill, I hood the face of my wedge to put more roll on my ball.

Another thing I do is vary the height and distance the ball travels by varying the amount my hands lead the clubhead through the ball. A lot of times you'll see Bill Casper or myself take a sand wedge and hit the ball only two feet off the ground. When the ball lands on the green, it takes one big bouncing skid and stops fast because it's got so much backspin on it. This backspin comes from

(A) I recommend using either a less lofted club or hooding the face of a wedge on an uphill shot. Downhill always use a lofted club. (B) You can vary the height of your pitch shots by the amount you keep your left hand ahead of the clubhead through the hitting area. (C) In situations where you need to stop the ball quickly, consciously try to keep the clubface open through the hitting area. (D) The more lofted the club, the harder it is to hit solid. With a sand wedge, the leading edge is under the ball before the face makes contact. A less lofted club puts the clubface squarely on the ball.

making a big lead of the hands into the ball, and pinching it at impact. To get less spin on the ball, reduce the lead of the hands so that you hit the ball almost like you would a putter, with the hands even with the ball at impact. The ball then "lobs" off the clubface with no spin whatsoever. On shots where I need to stop the ball extra quickly, I just keep the blade open through impact. This will put a trace of cut on the ball and stop it quickly.

The reason I'm discussing what I do on chipping is that I hope these things will be of help to advanced golfers who want to advance still further. But these are the kinds of shots that the average guy shouldn't even think about. He should just try to hit all his chips with the clubface square, and allow for the break as he would on a putt. He should also concentrate on hitting it solid. And, to help hit it solid, he should pick a club that is easy to hit solid.

To amplify this last point, let's compare what happens at impact when you hit a sand wedge and when you hit a 5-iron.

The leading edge of a sand wedge is already underneath the ball before the clubface hits the ball, but with a 5-iron you're putting the clubface squarely on the ball. So if you hit the 5-iron a little fat or thin, it's not going to hurt the chip much. But the more lofted the club, the harder it is to hit solid.

This is why I would discourage the average player from using wedges for most of his chip shots. Instead, he should use the least loft he can that will land the ball on the green and let it roll up to the hole.

Not that I think he should use every iron in the bag. That would make it too difficult. The best way is to standardize on just a few clubs and get to know them really well. As to what clubs, I think the 5-, 7-, and 9-irons would cover practically every situation. But I've seen some pretty good amateur chippers who use a 7-iron for just about every shot. The choice is really up to you.

As to the technique of the chip shot, I think basically you should keep the chip shot stroke as close to your putting stroke as possible. Play the ball off the left heel, with a narrow, slightly open stance, and choke down on the grip where it feels most comfortable,

The key to a good chipping action is to set up so that there is a perfect straight line from your left shoulder to the ball. Then, throughout the swing, simply maintain the straight line. This will prevent you from ever being too wristy, a common error on these short shots.

ideally so that only about an inch of grip shows. You should set up with the top of the grip level with the front of the ball on normal chips. In other words, the top of the handle will be level with the front of the ball. I make a point of setting up with my whole left arm and the club in a straight line down to the ball. During the stroke, I just try to maintain that straight line. This gives a firm, simple stroke with little wristiness.

The only time you should break your wrists a lot going back on a chip shot is when the lie isn't good. For example, when the ball is lying in thick fringe, you are going to have to pick the club up a little quicker in the backswing to get a more descending blow, just as I recommended on other shots from rough grass. However, if you have a good lie, and this of course is much of the time, you should just sweep the ball off the turf with a pendulum type stroke.

The biggest fault I see among amateurs on chipping is that they don't know their own chipping game. In other words, they have no idea how far to take it back to get the desired distance. And the reason for this is that their stroke is not consistent. Sometimes they use a little wrist, sometimes a lot of wrist. Keep the wrist action to a minimum and you will find your touch will improve rapidly. I should add that a swinging action will always result in some wrist movement. And if you eliminate all wrist action there will be no tempo and no smoothness.

The other fault I see is that most amateurs don't chip to a spot. To have a good chipping game you must aim to hit a spot. This is a necessary addition to your regular preshot checklist. You check all the variables and decide what type of chip to hit. Then you must pick the spot for the ball to land, and visualize the ball landing there and running up to the hole.

I'll take it further. If you don't visualize chipping to a spot, then you won't check what will happen when the ball lands, and as a result you're very often going to play the wrong shot. To give you an example of what I mean, on the final hole of the '74 World Open I faced a crucial little shot that would have meant the difference between tying Jack Nicklaus, Bob Murphy, and Frank Beard or finishing fourth. Although I was only thirty-five feet from the pin, I had some fringe to carry and only fifteen feet of green to work with —hardly an easy shot. The ball was sitting up nicely, so there was no need for a change in mechanics, but club selection was critical, as it turned out.

Initially, I fancied a shot that would land in the fringe and then roll to the hole. But when I checked the landing area, I saw that the grain in the Bermuda grass was running against me. So, instead of playing the less-lofted club I had at first visualized using, I took out a sand wedge, pitched onto the green about five feet short of the hole and watched the ball dance to a stop within "gimme" range.

I went on to win the playoff, but I wouldn't have been in it if I hadn't followed a thorough preshot mental checklist.

CHAPTER EIGHT

Sand Play Made Simple

To the average player, the sight of his ball veering in the direction of sand conjures up images of impending disaster. The reason is simple: If there's one shot that he almost invariably dubs, it's the sand shot.

The problem with such negative images is equally obvious. If you see yourself making a hash of every hole where you go in a bunker, then you'll continue to hit poor sand shots forever. In effect, you'll never get out of the beginner category in bunker play.

There's only one solution to the problem: You must have plenty of successful experiences in sand before you will feel comfortable in it. It's like the first few times that you rode a bicycle. At first it was awkward maintaining balance, and in addition you were a little worried you might fall off. But the more you rode, the more successful experiences you had riding, the better you became.

I've always had a lot of confidence in sand. And it's because in my early years in the game my dad had me practice bunker shots from every conceivable lie. You name it, I used to practice it. However, I should point out that I did learn the correct technique for every kind of shot, and that's very important. Perhaps more than any other shot, correct technique is at least half of the battle. Once you know the correct techniques, then the rest *is* practice. There's not a good bunker player in the world who hasn't at some point in his or her life spent long hours in the sand. There's really no short cut.

It is true that correct technique will get you out of the bunker, but without practice you probably won't be very close to the pin. And that's what I would like to see you aim for. If you can learn to chip well, then you *can* learn to play bunkers well, and that quality —especially in amateur play—is one that will make you feared as a player. If you can get it up and down from anywhere—including sand—you will be a match for anyone.

These days when I get into a trap, I'm just as confident I can turn three shots into two from there as anyplace else, more so sometimes. I'll give you an example of what I mean.

In the last round of the 1971 Crosby, on seventeen, I hit the purest shank you've ever seen into the woods on the right. I was stymied and had no shot to the green. Period. My only options were either to chip out to the fairway or into the bunker, which was some thirty yards closer to the green. Since I had more confidence in my sand play than in my short game, I chose the bunker, much to the amazement of the gallery. At this point in the round, I was either a stroke behind or tied for the lead with Jack Nicklaus, so I had to get the ball close to have a chance of winning. I knew that once I got over the ball I'd made the right decision, although I was still sixty-five feet from the flag. I lofted the ball out, it came down five feet in front of the hole, bit, ran round the lip of the hole and stayed out. A great bogey, but I was robbed! As it turned out, Jack three-putted the seventeenth, and we tied, but I lost to a birdie on the first hole of the playoff. Such is life.

I don't mean to sound as if I'm the best trap player on tour. I'm not. Certainly I'm not in the class of Chi Chi Rodriguez or Gary Player. Both have touch and technique that border sometimes on the unbelievable. But by tour standards, I'm more than adequate. One reason for this is that my swing method, as you'll see later in the chapter, adapts perfectly to sand with only minor changes.

The most basic of all rules in any trap situation is *get good footing*. Grind your shoes down until you feel the sand form a solid base beneath your feet. This prevents any chance of sinking in or sliding around while you're performing the stroke. While doing this, you also have the opportunity to get an idea of the texture and depth of the sand. Obviously, you can't touch the sand with the club without incurring a penalty, so your feet have to be the "feelers." Only when you know the density of the sand can you adapt your swing accordingly.

On all normal trap shots around the green, I recommend aiming for a spot two inches behind the ball. You can ensure hitting the spot by setting your head so that your eyes are centered over a spot two inches behind the ball.

I have never believed the theory that suggested you use the same length swing and vary the distance by the amount you hit behind the ball. It doesn't make sense. When you take a big swing and different amounts of sand, you'll get a big "nothing" shot that rolls a lot; there will be various amounts of spin on the ball. Whereas when you aim two inches behind the ball and vary the length of your swing, you'll get the same amount of backspin for the amount of force you use. You can use the spin to your advantage. That's why you see guys like Chi Chi toss shots right at the flag. He knows just how far to swing back on different-length shots. And he knows just how much force to apply to get enough backspin to stop the ball by the hole.

How you set up and swing in a trap is governed by the elements: the lie, the density of the sand, the height of the lip, how soft or hard the green is, and the distance from the ball to the flag. On a shorter shot, say, anywhere from fifteen to thirty-five feet from a greenside bunker that has reasonably soft sand, you should set up

(A) To make sure I hit the sand, I cock my head to the right so that my eyes are directly over a spot two inches behind the ball. (B) For an effective cutting action, the feet should be aligned open. The feeling that you want is that you are swinging the clubhead through parallel to your feet. However, the clubhead will still remain square to the target throughout.

more open than normal. The shorter the shot, the more open you should set up. This in itself will cause you to adopt a more upright plane, which, combined with an open clubface, will produce the most effective cutting action. On all shots from soft sand I advocate laying the clubface open. The softer the sand, the more open the face should be. By doing this you reduce the leading edge's cutting power by bringing into play the flange. The flange, or "bounce," as it is commonly known, is the part of the club that protrudes beneath the leading edge. The more you open the clubface, the more the flange comes into play. In soft sand the flange prevents the leading edge from cutting down too deeply under the ball. Instead of axing down steeply, the clubhead scythes through on a horizontal plane taking a limited amount of sand.

My swing method is ideal for sand, mainly because I already break my wrists in the take-away unconsciously. Remember how I told you that I fade the ball by creating the angle in my wrists? Well, on a regulation bunker shot that's what you have to do too. An early wrist break eliminates excessive wrist action or flippiness, at the top of the backswing, and gives you a little more leverage—pulling power—to get the clubhead through the sand. Then all you have to do after that is make sure that you don't release the angles until the ball has been struck. You do this by leading your left hand. Feel that you keep it in front of your right until after the ball is on its way. All this does is ensure that your wrists don't roll and that the clubhead moves through the sand on a horizontal plane. When the right hand turns over the left, it closes the face and causes the clubhead to dig deeper. *You must keep the clubface open in soft sand.* I simply cannot stress enough the importance of this. My father used to make me imagine that I had a glass balanced on the clubface. The only way it could stay there was if the clubface remained open through the hitting area.

Another useful image, and the same principle I use on a regular short shot from the grass, is imagining that the path the clubhead follows through impact (the swing line) parallels the foot line. In other words, try to swing in the direction your feet are aiming. If the

The early set of the wrists is essential for leverage to cut down and through the sand.

Try to keep the clubhead open through the hitting area. A good mental image to help accomplish this is picturing a glass balanced on the face. If the clubface closed, the glass would fall off.

clubface is wide open, as it should be, even though the swing line does parallel the foot line the ball is going to go where the clubface is aimed. The ball will still fly at the pin because the face is square. I should add that, because of the cutting action, you should aim the clubface a hair left of the hole to allow for a natural left-to-right spin tendency. When the ball lands, the spin is going to make the ball jump to the right.

PLAYING FROM HARD SAND

In most cases hard sand is wet sand. But this also includes bunkers with very little sand and a hard base of, say, one to two

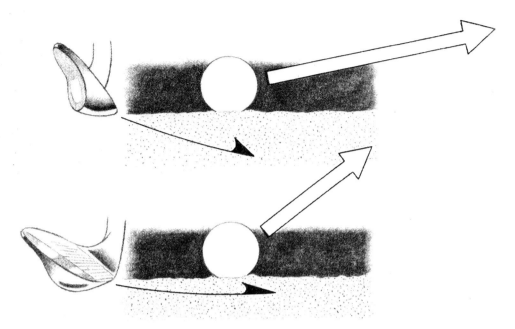

When you close the clubface in hard sand, the leading edge comes into play and gives you additional cutting power. In soft sand, however, the leading edge should be eliminated by turning the face open. Then the depth the clubhead travels under the ball will be shallower.

inches. You can tell quite readily that it's hard by the depth that you are able to grind your feet down when taking your stance. Here, the leading edge of the wedge is your biggest helper. Instead of opening the face you must square it up. The last thing you want is an open face, because should the flange contact the hard sand, the club could bounce right off the surface into the ball, and you'd skull the shot clear over the green. With the face square you'll be using the leading edge to your advantage.

Other than this relatively simple fundamental change, the swing is the same as if you were playing a regulation wedge shot. However, you don't need to swing quite as hard. Because with a square clubface you have less loft, the ball will come out lower and roll more. Remember, you're using more force, so be sure to allow for more backspin and toss the ball right to the hole.

BURIED LIES AND OTHER TROUBLE

In the last round of the 1971 Masters, my tee shot on the short twelfth buried in the face of the bunker, leaving me about thirty feet to the flag. I was four under at the time, two back of the leaders, and very much in contention. I had a plugged, uphill lie—strictly a red light situation. Scary. I certainly wasn't about to open the face up and play it like a normal shot. I got in the trap, *closed* up the face, slightly lifted my left shoulder to offset the upslope, and thumped the sand with as much force as I could muster without looking like a gorilla. The ball pitched fifteen feet from the flag and ran straight in the hole like a putt. Buried lies aren't always as easy to handle, but with a thorough understanding of the situations they can be coped with.

How much the ball is buried always designates the clubface position you'll ultimately want to use; for example, if the ball is only partially buried—half up, half down—I suggest that the clubface be square and you use the same swing as for hard sand. But if the ball is deep, barely showing above the surface, then *the clubface should be closed.* Your stance should be just about square to compensate for this, and the ball slightly to the right of the normal left heel position by about an inch. This along with a conscious effort to take the club back outside the line will produce a steeper downswing arc. A normal release of the angles in the right arm is mandatory, but added force isn't. The closed clubface position will do all the work for you. Just aim for the point where the plug starts, the back of the rim, in other words, and make sure the leading edge gets under the ball. The ball will fly out very low, with forward spin on it, and run like a scared rabbit. No one except maybe Chi Chi has ever been able to get any backspin from a plugged lie.

UPHILL DOWNHILL

All of the fundamentals that I outlined in Chapter Six apply here. One other point, though, is that on an uphill lie you'll want to use a lot more force. Because of the slope and the fact that you're hitting up on the ball, trying to parallel the slope, in other words, the ball is going to fly higher but a lot less distance. I use the image that the pin is an extra ten or fifteen feet farther back to overcome any tendency to leave the ball short.

On downhill lies, you'll want to move the ball back an inch to the right of the left heel. This, again, to ensure that you have a steep downswing arc and contact the sand a little closer to the ball. You'll find that the ball will fly a lot lower, so you'll be wise to open the clubface a little.

A vital key on uphill and downhill lies is to make your downswing arc through the ball parallel the slope. You do this by adjusting the position of your shoulders at address. On the uphill lie you raise your left shoulder a little and lower the right. Hitting downhill, you do the opposite—lower your left shoulder and raise the right.

SIDEHILL (above and below feet)

Here again most of the short game fundamentals apply. However, I must touch upon one or two points that differ slightly. For example, when the ball is below your feet, grip up the shaft and make a concerted effort to stay down and hit the sand. You can expect the shot to move right, so initially align yourself, as much as the limitations of the slope will allow, slightly to the left of the flag.

The reverse is true when the ball is above your feet. It will move to the left. To compensate for this, choke up on the club, set your feet square and the clubface only *slightly* open, and set your hands in a lower position so that the toe of the club doesn't grab at impact.

ON LONG SHOTS

My effective range with a sand wedge, hitting two inches behind the ball, goes to about thirty yards. Beyond this I drop down

to a pitching wedge or, if the sand is really fluffy, an 8- or 9-iron. Like on the twelfth hole at Doral in 1975, I had a sixty-yard shot of semifluffy sand. A sand wedge was out of the question and a pitching wedge was too much of a risk; I'd have to strike the ball first, and if I didn't I'd hit fat. So I took an 8-iron, hit about an inch and a half behind, and knocked the ball stiff. This shot was largely a matter of experience. It was one that I'd played several times before and one that I had confidence I could repeat. But I chose the shot because it gave me the most room for error. It was an option. You have similar options. Just because you have, say, fifty to sixty yards to the flag, it doesn't mean you have to use a sand wedge. Many times a pitching wedge or other short iron will do a better job. That's important to remember.

I would like to make a couple of additional technical points on these longer bunker shots. Unless you're close to the front lip and need great height on the shot, you don't need to open the face as much as on the shorter shots. A slightly open face is usually all that is required. Also, to obtain the necessary distance, you will often have to hit closer in back of the ball than the two inches I recommended for the greenside bunker shots.

THE FAIRWAY BUNKER

This is not an easy shot by any standards. I suggest standing slightly taller, with a little less flex in your knees. This will help you hit the ball first, not the sand. Also the clubface should be turned open slightly to encourage height to get up over the front of the bunker. In the swing itself, try to keep the left hand leading for as long as possible by delaying the release of the angles. If your right

With an uphill or downhill lie in the sand, the trick is to make the club-head follow the contour of the slope. To accomplish this, you lower your left shoulder and raise your right when playing downhill. And, uphill, raise the left shoulder and lower the right.

hand dominates, then likely you'll hit the sand rather than the ball first.

Above all, be sure to get a good footing. Otherwise, you'll be making a big swing on shaky ground, and anything could happen. Then, don't try to overswing or try for too much distance. Swing smoothly.

The Philosophical Approach

Some years back Grier Jones, who has always been a super trap player, told me that when he gets in sand he always looks to play the shot that will get him out. In other words, he doesn't want to attempt *any* shot where the ball might stay in the trap. This I think is the best philosophical approach for everybody. You've just got to say "What's the easiest way to get the ball on the green?" If you have a bad lie, then you better take the easy way and hit a shot you know will get you on the green. If the ball is lying well and you have confidence in your ability, then you can maybe go ahead and try to get it close. It's like the red, yellow, and green situation, you have to be realistic. Not every bunker shot is equally tough. Some you can't wait to hit because you just know the ball is going to finish close. Then there are others where the odds aren't too good and you have to be realistic and play accordingly.

I got in a situation at the U. S. Open in 1974 that actually opened my eyes to Grier's theory. I'd hit my second shot on the seventh hole at Winged Foot into possibly the deepest bunker on the course on the right hand side of the green. The pin was tucked over in the right corner, which left me a shot of about fifteen feet with no green to work with. But, to get close, I had to land the ball just over the lip and let it roll down to the hole. I was overconfident and unrealistic. Three times the ball caught the top of the lip and rolled back at my feet. Finally, I realized I was attempting the impossible and wedged out past the flag. Touch wood, I won't make the same mistake again.

CHAPTER NINE

The Natural Way to Putt

Putting is a lot like pitching pennies into a cup, it requires more "feel" than technique. When you toss a penny you're not considering how you're tossing it, only *where* you're tossing it. Putting is the same way. The second you think technique, once you're over the ball, you're crowding your conscious mind with unnecessary thoughts. These will clog the spontaneous reaction that comes initially from your subconscious mind, and prevent your muscles from getting an accurate read-out on how hard to hit the putt. Like the full shot swing, putting technique must be developed on the practice green and be second nature on the course.

In reality, a putting stroke is just a miniature golf swing. If you watch any player, a good player or a hacker, I guarantee you'll see the exact same physical characteristics in both the full swing and the putting stroke. For example, I have never seen a guy with a

Putting is like pitching pennies: It requires more feel than technique.

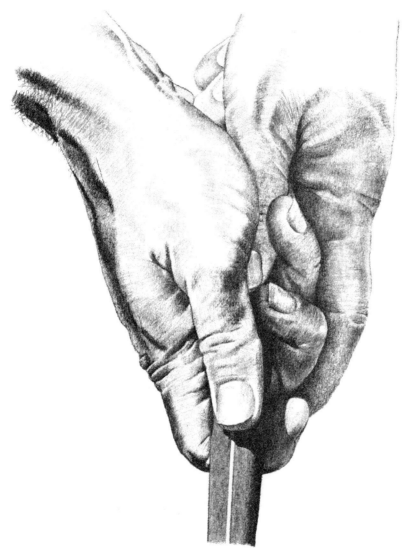

Like in the full swing, the grip that I advocate on the green is the palm-to-palm. The only difference is that the index finger of the left hand runs down the first three fingers of the right. This puts all the fingers of the right hand on the shaft, which I believe is where all the sensitivity lies.

superfast backswing use a superslow putting stroke. Or vice versa. Jack Nicklaus starts the club away from the ball very deliberately with his driver and does the same thing with his putter. Bob Murphy has that lovely long slow swing and has a beautifully slow putting stroke. My stroke, too, has the exact same tempo as my swing, and even has the slight pause at the top, between my backswing and downswing.

The fundamentals, also, are nearly identical. My grip, for example, is a basic palm-to-palm grip, the main difference being that I reverse overlap. The index finger of my left hand runs down the first three fingers of my right. This, like the regular overlapping, gets the hands close together. It also places *all* the fingers of the right hand, and specifically the fingertips, on the grip. This is important because the right hand is where all the sensitivity lies.

In putting, my right thumb, like my left, is placed straight down the middle of the grip. However, the same separation exists between the index and the middle fingers as in my regular grip. This placement of the thumb and forefinger gives you maximum feel. In just about every sport that involves throwing, these two act as the "feelers." They do the bulk of the work in gauging distance. A surgeon holds his scalpel with his forefinger and thumb, a writer his pen, and so on. Under no circumstances should any pressure, *ever*, be applied in these two; instead, they should just rest on the grip.

As regards stance, I set my feet a little inside shoulder width. My weight favors my left side, to prevent head movement. I also prefer to stand slightly open on the green, because it gives me a better perspective of the line to the hole. Standing closed, my view of the line is partially blocked by my left side, which makes it awkward to retain a clear picture of the line. You can see, so far, that all these fundamentals are the same as used in the full swing.

The angle created where the back of the left hand and wrist are joined must remain constant throughout the stroke for the putterhead to be square.

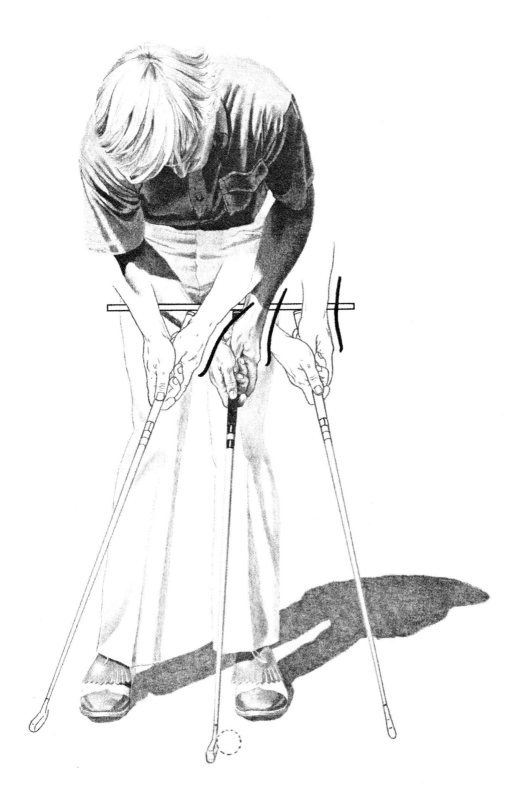

The ball position also doesn't change; the ball is placed directly off the left heel. My hands, in relation to the ball, are placed a little forward so that the top of the grip is level with the front of the ball. As in a full swing if the hands are behind the ball, the hands will be unable to work as a unit, and the right hand will tend to dominate.

You must remember that a key thought in my swing theory was the angle at the back of the hand and wrist. *If the angle remains constant, then you'll be square.* The exact same thing applies in putting. The angle created where the wrist and hand meet should be clearly visible when you look down at your hands, and remain constant during your stroke.

Putting styles are as varied and as individual as golf swings. Some people prefer to crouch over the ball; others stand more erect. I personally tend to go with the former, because I like to get my eyes right over the ball. In reality, my dominant left eye, because the ball is positioned off the left heel, looks directly at the back of the ball. My eyes, however, are right over the line to the hole.

In the golf swing, when you bend from the waist, you'll tend to adopt an upright plane. It's the same in the putting stroke. To develop more of a true pendulum-type action where the blade stays on the line longer, you must bend forward enough so that the arms and shoulders *can* work in pendulum fashion. Remember: The longer the putterhead is on line through the contact area, the better your chances of a square strike. Also, make sure your hands are held in a fairly upright position initially; again, the blade will stay on the line better. If you stand too erect with your upper body, or have your hands too low, then the natural tendency will be to draw the putter back inside the line too much, making square contact much more chancy.

My whole thesis on putting has very little to do with the putt-

I prefer a slightly open stance because it gives me a better ball-hole perspective. Also, I get a more solid strike by setting my eyes directly over the ball.

erhead. I feel that the putter can only do what your hands allow. If your hands do a good job, the putterhead will too. Because of this, once the putter has been aligned "square," at right angles to the hole, I focus my attention on making sure that the hands do what they are supposed to.

You may remember, when talking about the take-away in the full swing, I said too many players are clubhead oriented. The same thing applies in putting. For decades now, people have been taught that the putterhead must stay low to the ground throughout the stroke. This is correct in that the clubhead *will* stay low to the ground in a good stroke. The problems arise when golfers try to *force* the club to stay low.

If you were to imagine a line running across the top of the grip, horizontally, and then go ahead and try to keep the putterhead low by pushing the blade down and away from the ball, then down and through to the hole, you'll see that the top of the grip "dips" way below the line both on the backswing and follow-through. How can you be consistent when the top of the grip is bobbing up and down like a fishing float? There is just no way you'll hit the ball solidly all the time. My feeling is that the top of the grip should stay on a level plane throughout the stroke. This applies to anyone regardless of whether he has wrist or arm-oriented strokes.

Billy Casper, undoubtedly one of the finest "wrist" putters in the world, keeps the top of the grip on the same plane by setting his left hand solidly against the inside of his left thigh. Of course he'd never admit it. I remember telling him about my theory on the top of the grip, and about his stroke. His response, jokingly, was "Go back to what you were doing. Don't start what I'm doing. I don't want anybody doing that!" But he does keep the grip on that level plane. And that, I feel, is one of the keys to his success.

Logically, the easiest way you keep the top of the grip on the level plane is through a pendulum action of your hands and arms rather than the wrists. Overuse of the wrists, unless like Casper you stick your left wrist against your thigh, will cause the top of the grip to dip.

This is why my stroke, and the method I advocate, involves use of 85 to 90 per cent hands and arms. Also, the less wrist you use, the fewer moving parts there are, and with fewer moving parts, there is less likelihood for error.

If you watch most of golf's best putters, you'll find that they are basically hand-arm putters. Few are wristy, with the exception of Casper and Arnold Palmer.

Through use of the hands and arms, you develop more of a pendulum-type action where the shoulders rotate slightly. However, despite what a lot of experts say—that the best putters are "arm-shoulder" putters—this shoulder rotation is just a result of your arms making the stroke. The term "arm-shoulder" putter, which is used

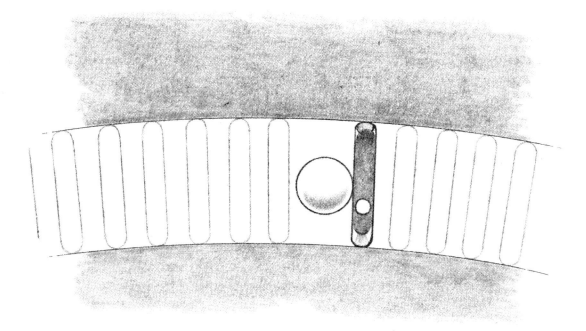

In a hand-arm stroke, which is what I recommend, there is a gradual opening and closing of the blade. The putterhead follows a half-moon shape first around the right side and then the left. In technical terminology, an "inside-to-inside" stroke. To ensure a consistently solid strike, try to feel that you are keeping the top of the grip on a level plane throughout the stroke.

frequently in golf instruction articles, I believe is misleading, because it implies conscious shoulder rotation. Conscious shoulder rotation is a necessity on the fairway, but it isn't on the green—unless
you're on one of those double greens at St. Andrews! The hands are
the leaders in the putting stroke. The arms and the shoulders only
work in response to the hands. From hands to arms to shoulders, it's
all a chain reaction.

The key, I believe, is to develop a stroke where the hands and
the clubhead follow a half-moon-shaped arc around first the right
side and then the left side. In technical terminology, this is an inside-to-inside stroke, the putterhead going back inside the line on
the backswing and back to the inside in the follow-through. However, the putterhead remains on the line for a few inches in the take-
away and also for a few inches both before and after contact. I am
not suggesting this should be a conscious move; it will happen as a
result of the shoulder rotation in the hand-arm stroke. Unless you
consciously force the hands to do otherwise, they will naturally take
the putterhead back and through in this half-moon shape. One other
interesting point that should be made here is that, the closer you
stand to the ball, the longer the blade will stay on the link. Obviously then, the farther away you stand, the more inside to inside the
blade will go.

A hand-arm stroke also involves what appears to be a gradual
opening and closing of the clubface. If you were to give a putter to a
kid who had never putted before or played before in his life, you'd
see that he would naturally let the putterface open and close in relation to the target line like a gate. He would do this unconsciously.
However, this opening and closing of the blade is an illusion. It is
caused by the rotation of the shoulders in the backswing and follow-
through. At all times the putterface remains square to the shoulder
line. Many people fall into the error of thinking that the blade must
stay square to the line throughout the stroke. In forcing the clubface
to stay on the line, they create a shut-to-open type, wristy stroke. Although there are some players who use this type of method success-
fully, it is, I'm convinced, a manufactured move for the greater ma-

jority of players. I feel in the long run a more natural putting method will stand up the longest.

I remember when I was in college, and playing a lot with Mike Taylor, who was then the number one player on the Brigham Young team, and a great putter, I copied his shut-to-open stroke. For about a year I putted like a wizard, but then the roof caved in. I couldn't make a putt from any distance. It took me quite a while to readapt to my old hand-arm stroke, but eventually my touch returned.

My suspicions have also been confirmed on the tour by the amount of streaky open-to-close putters there are knocking about. One minute they have twenty-seven putts a round, the next thirty-six. The best way to putt is the natural way, the hand-arm, open-to-close method, just like in the full swing.

Everything we have discussed so far is for one purpose: to strike the ball solidly with the putter, consistently.

Anytime you hit the ball solid you're hitting it in the middle of the clubface, so you can't go too far wrong. The putts that miss, or come up short most of the time, are the ones hit on the toe or heel.

In developing a solid stroke I am very much an advocate of a short backstroke and a long follow-through. Ideally, I'd recommend 45 per cent backstroke, 55 per cent follow-through. The shorter the backstroke, the less room for error. The longer the follow-through, the more acceleration there'll be in the stroke and thus less likelihood that you'll "quit," that is, stop once the ball has been struck. To "quit," you have to start to quit long before the putterface ever contacts the ball; you decelerate somewhere in the downswing. Acceleration, just as in the full swing, is a necessity. This applies on all putts. You can ensure acceleration by making a smooth take-away. Any "jerkiness" creates premature acceleration, and the instinctive reaction is to slow down in the downswing.

ESTABLISHING YOUR TEMPO ON THE GREEN

As I said before, the tempo of your stroke will generally match your swing tempo, unless, of course, you're consciously trying to change it—either speed it up or slow it down. Either will do you no good at all. It's unnatural for someone who has used a fast stroke for five years to go out and say, "Today I'm going to start the putt-erhead away from the ball very deliberately," and expect results in one day. He's got no chance. And the same is true for someone who has a slow stroke. You have to establish *your* own tempo. If it's fast, or slow, fine. Just be sure you know your own tempo. Then when you are under pressure you'll have a better chance of avoiding drastic changes in tempo.

I found out, fortunately, that one of my habits under extreme pressure was speeding up. In other words, when I had maybe the lead in a tournament, or was in contention, I would tend to start thinking and walking faster. The more pressure, the faster I'd walk, which caused my putting stroke to get jerky. Today, I've learned to pace myself and I feel I can play down to the wire as well as anyone. Something that has helped me in this respect is never losing sight of the one critical element, which is the first thing to depart when you start to "choke": tempo.

Coming down to the wire, you know, the mind races. You get over a putt and you start thinking in terms of "could" and "should." "If I could make this putt I'll win the tournament." Or, "If I should happen to miss this . . ." You have to keep these thoughts out of your head, because they distract you from making a smooth stroke. You fall into the trap of wanting to get the putt over with, and speed up.

I've found a method of keeping my stroke smooth and well timed under pressure, which can be applied, with practice, to your stroke, too. It's a count of One . . . Two. The backswing is One, I have that slight pause at the top . . . then the downswing is Two. So all I'll do when I'm faced with a critical putt is make one stroke first to establish the tempo, then just apply a count to it. A second practice putt registers the over-all speed in my mind and I just carry it right into stroking the putt. The longer the putt, the slower the count. As I say, this "One . . . Two" count fits my stroke perfectly, but you must establish your own tempo. It could be One . . . Two, or One . . . Two . . . Three, or some other count. Whatever the count you settle on, I think it's a terrific way of handling pressure putts.

ON READING GREENS

Good putters are good greens readers. And a good greens reader is a patient man. I don't mean to sound as though I am encouraging slow play, I'm not. But I think one of the principal problems among average players is that they don't absorb all the elements. The more you take in, the better your chance of making the putt.

When you see pros stalking around the hole, like Sherlock Holmes hot on the scent of a clue, it's because they know that even the smallest undulation or change in grain, the direction in which the grass runs, will have a marked effect on the way the ball rolls. Sometimes you get practice putts that defy the law of averages. They look like they'll break one way and then break the other. There is usually a reason for it, hidden in the way the grain runs, or some slight undulation. However, you have to know what you're looking for to see it.

Before a tournament round, during practice, you will often see pros putt to various imaginary pin placements around a green. This enables them to get to know even the smallest subtleties; the speed of the green; the way the grain runs in different areas; and of course the way the green breaks. If there are certain abnormalities on a particular green, they'll be recorded on the scorecard as a reminder to the player during the tournament.

Break is, to me, relatively easy to read. There are times, especially on courses in flat areas, where I can be temporarily baffled, but most of the time I'm pretty accurate. As to how I read it, I'll get down, directly behind the ball, and look back along an imaginary line from my ball to the hole. This low viewpoint enables me to see the break, most of the time.

Occasionally, if the break is subtle, I'll use the plumb bob method. I'll hold the putter by the middle of the grip and let it hang, vertically, in front of my left eye so that the shaft dissects the hole. This way I can see any break on either side of the cup. Only rarely do I ever walk to the opposite side of the hole and look back at the line. I think you almost invariably get a better perspective of the line from directly behind the putt. Occasionally Andy Martinez might go to the opposite side for me, just to verify any decision we have made. It gives me a lot of confidence to know that he sees the putt breaking the same way I do.

Andy also helps me in that, if he sees an error made during the stroke, he'll observe it and tell me afterward. Or, if he sees something happen to the ball somewhere along the line that we hadn't allowed for, he'll point it out. All these things help me to understand my own stroke and the elements better.

When Andy is not with me, I go through virtually all the same things in my own head. If I miss a putt, I don't want to say, "O.K., I've missed it," and walk to the next tee. I want to know *why* I've missed it. If I could feel the fault in my stroke, fine. I'll work on that at the corner of the green for a minute. But if it was something that I missed in the line, then I'll go on a "search and destroy" mission. Only after I find that missing link will I have peace of mind. I'll also have enhanced my knowledge and know what to look for the next time around.

Average players would do well to do the same thing. For example, I see this all the time: A guy misses a putt and stalks off the green like he's just had his favorite toy stolen, without ever questioning why. As a result, he'll get down on himself to the point where he won't make another putt for the rest of the round. One thing to remember is that a machine on a good green makes a ten-footer only 60 per cent of the time. The cause isn't always your stroke, it could be the grain. If you don't ever look back and check to see, then you'll never know and will never improve. It doesn't take a second to look back over the line. Then next time you'll remember.

One of the best gimmicks that I've come up with, over the

years, to gauge both break and grain, is to imagine I am pouring a bucket of water on top of the grass. Then I'll just picture which way the water runs. Not only is that the way the green breaks, but 99 per cent of the time it's the way the grain runs. I've found that grain goes mostly with the contour of the green and the way the drainage goes. Grain is more predominant in Bermuda grass, a wiry strain that is found mainly south of the continental divide, in the warmest climates. Bermuda has a rather unique habit: It follows the sun. As the sun rises in the morning, so does the grass. At night it lies down again. So you'll find that the grain is less pronounced in the morning than later in the day. The grain always lies the way the sun sets. That's more west in summer and more southwest in winter.

Bent grass is a much softer-textured grass, which is found mostly in the Midwest and Northern states and also on seaside courses in the West. Being softer, grain in Bent has a lesser effect on the way the ball rolls. However, it is still a factor in determining which way a putt will break. Because of its close-knit formation Bent grain is a lot harder to read than Bermuda, although the same principles do apply.

To most players the easiest way to read grain would be to look down and see which way the grass is leaning. If it's leaning toward you, it would be against and would mean you'd have to hit the putt harder; to the left or right obviously the ball will move in that direction, and if it's leaning away from you then you can expect the ball to roll fairly straight and must allow for more speed accordingly. Unfortunately, it's not always that easy to read and other methods must be called into use.

The most common method is to look for light or dark patches in the green. If you see, between the ball and the hole, that the grass is light and shiny, then the grain is going away from you. In other words, leaning toward the hole. The shine is created by the sun's reflection on the top side of the freshly clipped grass. When there is a dark patch it means the grain is leaning against you. Like the front of a crew-cut hair style, the grass has been forced upward so that the underside of it shows.

141

I could go on, but the subject of grain by itself could almost take a book to cover. I have outlined what I believe to be the most important aspects of reading break and grain. Neither should be taken for granted. And for anyone who doubts the importance of grain especially, consider this analogy: If you were an ant crossing a green, your journey would hardly be smooth; it would be like crossing the Himalayan mountain range! Even though a golf ball is a lot bigger than an ant, only a small part of the ball comes into contact with the grass. So, although a green may look as smooth as a billiard table, there are always hidden obstacles—hidden, that is, unless you get down and take a close look. That's why a machine makes only four out of ten ten-foot putts.

THE MENTAL SIDE OF PUTTING

To make any length putt not only requires a good stroke and an understanding of the putting surface, it requires the belief that you can make it. And it requires the ability to concentrate.

Concentration means focusing solely on the elements that will provide you with a successful outcome, which is hard work because there is a lot involved. But without concentration there is no way you can putt well.

Let me show you what goes through my mind before and during a putt. As I said, when I first get to the ball, I get down behind and establish the line the ball will follow. I do this through visualization. I literally "see" the ball traveling down a line to the hole. On breaking putts many players establish a line, then pick out a spot at a point where the ball is likely to break and where it should enter the hole. I prefer to visualize the whole line. When you have a

I am not a believer in spot putting, picking a spot between the ball and the hole over which the ball should travel. I prefer visualizing the total line to the hole.

spot plus the hole, it becomes mentally exhausting to focus on both. Once the line has been established, I next visualize the stroke, the length, and the tempo that will send the ball the required distance. Lastly, I see the ball leaving the putterface, traveling down the line, and falling into the hole. As Jack Nicklaus says, it's like going to the movies. If I can get these pictures transferred from my conscious mind to my subconscious mind, then there is every chance the read-out I get will be accurate and I'll make the putt.

You can see that most of the *heavy* thinking is done prior to the putt being made. During the physical act of stroking the ball, I'm conscious of nothing and aware of everything. I rarely use physical keys other than the tempo count I told you about earlier. The freer my mind is, the easier it will be to allow a spontaneous reaction. Conscious thought is inhibiting. Can you imagine a basketball player shooting and thinking how he was going to shoot at the same time? Impossible. The reason he makes baskets is not because he's keying on something physical. His mind just focuses on the basket. Because he's experienced making the same type of shot before and has seen the ball disappear through the hoop many times, his subconscious mind just gives a read-out to his muscles on how hard to throw the ball. He knows that, having done it before, he can do it again. That's what it really boils down to in putting: To make putts you have to first experience making them. The only way you can do that is through practice. And you look at any tournament sight, you'll see more pros on the putting green than anywhere else. Experiencing.

You hear about people who have putting "streaks." I'm convinced that you make a lot of putts only if you start out making a lot of putts. This isn't always true but most of the time it is. On the first few holes you hole one or two, say, ten-footers. So your subconscious mind gets tuned in on seeing the ball go in the hole. Your conscious mind meanwhile develops the attitude that anything is possible and, before you know it, you're holing everything. Arnold Palmer a few years back got into a serious putting slump and completely lost his confidence. One day he spent a whole afternoon on the putting green holing one-foot putts. He thus refamiliarized his mind with seeing the ball go in the hole and his touch returned.

If you follow golf at all, you'll know that Bobby Nichols has a knack for holing putts in "clutch" situations to win big money tournaments. Although I've never asked him about this, I remember watching him once or twice when he pulled off the impossible. At the Dow Jones a few years back, I was playing with him in the final group, and he needed a long putt on the last green. I remember watching his actions as he moved in to make his stroke. Everything was positive. It was apparent that there was no doubt in his mind that he'd make the putt. When he hit the ball I thought to myself, "There is no way that ball will get to the hole," it was going so slowly, it looked as if it would be a foot short. Then I heard Bobby say, "Get in," and it did. He almost willed it into the hole. Another time at the Westchester Classic, Bobby arrived on the last tee needing an eagle three to tie Bob Murphy and force a playoff. He knew it too, and laced two shots onto the par-5 eighteenth green and then holed for an eagle. And to show you the power of positive thinking, on the first playoff hole he did the exact same thing for a birdie and first place money! Having experienced similar things myself, solely because of visualization, I have to believe that programming positive thought is the key to putting well. That means completely eliminating the negative and focusing only on good things.

At Greensboro in 1975 in the first round of the tournament, I was putting just average. I couldn't make any birdie putts but I wasn't three putting. So right after the round I was called into the press tent and went through my round with the press, telling them what club I hit on each hole and how long the putts were, etc. I made a comment during this time that my putting stroke had gone sour and I couldn't make anything. The next day my golf improved but my putting didn't. Toward the end of the second round, however, Tom Shaw, whom I was playing with, came up to me and said, "I've been watching your stroke and there is absolutely nothing wrong with it." That gave me confidence and I started to putt reasonably well again. I got to thinking, "Maybe if I say there is nothing wrong with my stroke and start working on positive action I'll putt better." Needless to say that's exactly what happened. The next two days I putted super, carried the same feeling **right** into the Masters the following week, and finished second.

The lesson to be learned from my experience is a simple one: If you miss a few putts, don't ever get down on yourself. Forget it. This is undoubtedly one of the hardest things to do. Most players are still thinking about the negatives, like a putt missed back on the first hole when they're home watching the football game on TV, cringing through every minute of it. A good putter becomes a good putter because he remembers the putts he makes, not the ones he misses. A bad putter does just the opposite. If you tell yourself you can't putt, you never will because you're programming and visualizing failure. But program exactly what you want to do, and visualize the putts dropping—and they will!

CHAPTER TEN

On Playing Percentage Golf

There are stories around the tour that Ben Hogan used to preplan his rounds on a blackboard in his motel room before a tournament. Whether that's true or not I don't know. I do know, however, that the great players have always been great planners and that a sound game plan is as essential in golf as it is in football. A football coach certainly wouldn't advance his team far without a plan. The opposing team would run right over him. It's the same in golf, except that the opposing team in this case is the golf course. And believe me, any good course can have as much ferocity as a 220-pound linebacker if you just hit and hope.

To play good golf, you have to be prepared and preprogram yourself. I know I do most of my heavy thinking prior to a round. I'll review each hole in my mind, pick targets for each shot, and go over the type of shots I will hit. In short, I'll play the round ahead of time in my mind. It's like plotting a route on a map. You know where you're going, but unless you know the route and exit numbers before you start, you're liable to take a few scenic but unwanted detours.

In mapping out the course, my first consideration is the yardage. In fact, the very first thing I do when I arrive at a tournament site is to pace off the course with Andy's help. We do it in sections—just like a football field. On par-4's, we'll select a convenient landmark such as a tree or sprinkler head in the center of the fairway close to where my tee shot will finish, and then pace off the yardage from that point to the front, the middle, and the back of the green. This way, wherever the pin is placed on any given day, I'll know the exact yardage. On par-5's we'll only pace off the yardage from a point about a hundred yards out from the green. There's no necessity to pace off the first part of the hole because in most cases it will take two good wood shots. The only exception, of course, would be if I had to lay up in front of some hazard or other. Then on the par-3's, we step off the yardage from the back of the tee to the front, center, and back of the green. If the tees are placed forward, then it is simply a matter of pacing off the yardage from the back of the tee to the tee marker and subtracting this figure from the total yardage figure we have to arrive at the distance.

Incidentally, I wonder how many amateurs really know the yardages at their home course, and when I say yardages I mean exact yardages down to the last yard. I'll bet it's less than 10 per cent of the membership of any club, and those would be the low-handicappers! Yet pacing off the course would only take an afternoon or two and is in many ways the first step to successful strategy. In so doing you are forced to really think your way around the course. You determine the holes that have been giving you problems, and can figure out where you've been going wrong, be it bad club selection or other mental errors.

Of course I should point out that knowing the exact yardages on your course is going to be useful to you only *if* you know your personal distances with each club. So, if you don't know exactly your range of distances with each club, go out to the practice tee one time and find out! Maybe you can't play like a professional, but you owe it to yourself and your game to think like one. Remember: You can't make a realistic club selection unless you have these two basics—the exact yardage and the distances you can hit with each club.

While I'm pacing off the course, I'll also be scouting for suitable landing areas for my tee shots. You get some fairways that look perfectly flat from the tee, but when you get out to your drive you find you've got a sidehill lie. So it's essential to know where you want the ball to land. But there's another reason for establishing a landing area, and that is you must have a target clearly established in your mind for every shot you hit, and that includes tee shots. Even though I'm going to explain this matter of "target" in detail, I have to mention it here, because I see so many amateurs who just tee it high and let it fly. As a result, their tee shots can and do go anywhere. Hitting a golf ball without establishing a target makes as much sense as aiming a gun with your eyes closed.

If the fairway slopes one way or other in the landing area, this will dictate the type of shot you should play from the toe—a draw or a fade. When the fairway slopes from right to left, use the slope to your advantage by playing a draw and getting additional roll on the ball. If the fairway slopes the other way, play a fade. The only exception to this strategy is if the slope is extreme and there is trouble on the low side. Then you'd play a fade into the right-to-left slope and a draw into the left-to-right slope to prevent the ball from running down the slope too much.

For the most part, though, it is the design of the hole you're playing that dictates the type of tee shot you should play. In practice I always ask myself, "What kind of hole is this, and how does the designer want me to play it?" Then, I'll see what is the best route to the green. If the hole is not too long, maybe I won't want to hit a driver at all, but instead take a fairway wood or long iron. Then you have to consider the trouble. For example, if there are a lot of good bunkers in the landing area of a good-length drive, consider

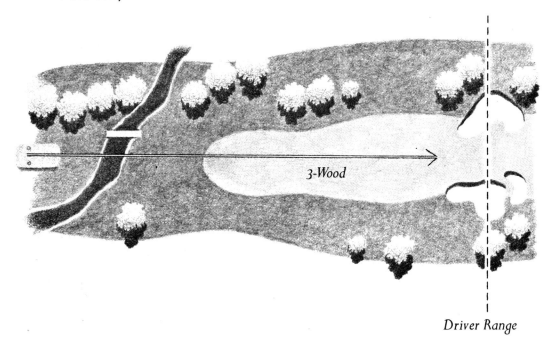

3-Wood

Driver Range

If there is a lot of trouble in the landing area, it often pays to drop from a driver to a 3-wood. This type of decision should be dictated by the amount of club you would be left with into the green.

laying up short of them with a fairway wood. But if the bunkers will only catch a *poor* drive, you will usually find it pays to try and carry them. If you were to lay up short, you would usually find yourself trying to hit the green with too long a club. In other words, if the hole is designed by the architect as a drive and a 5-iron for the average player, and if you were to lay up, you would find that the 2-iron you would then have to take for your second shot would not hold the green. Laying up then would be overcautious. The key to the tee shot really is to remember that what you're doing is setting up your second shot. It's one thing to hit a safe tee shot, but if it doesn't set up a good second shot for you, it's no good. When there is trouble on one side of the hole, I don't believe in the old theory that you should aim toward the trouble and then try to curve the ball away from it.

150

To my way of thinking, this is a bunch of hogwash. For example, let's say there is an out-of-bounds on the left and you set up aimed toward the out-of-bounds intending to fade the ball back to the fairway. Suppose you hit it straight? That's right, the ball will go straight O.B. My point is you have to have no room for error by hitting it to the left. In this situation, my strategy would be to start the ball down the *right* side of the hole and plan to draw the ball back into the fairway. Even if the shot doesn't come off as intended, you still have plenty of room for error. If you hit it straight or even fade it, the worst that will happen is that you are in rough on the right. A slight draw means, of course, you're in the fairway. The only way that you can go O.B. is if you snap hook it. And I think three out of four chances isn't bad—it's certainly better than one out of two!

If you're still unconvinced, let's consider another example. Suppose there is a water hazard on the left side out maybe 190 yards from the tee. Now, with the old theory you'd set up left, aligned straight at the hazard. Again, instead of hitting the ball with a fade, you might easily hit it dead straight—splash—into the water. The water hazard rule says you must drop behind the point of entry and take a stroke penalty. If you hit the ball straight into the hazard, that point of entry is going to be close to the front of the hazard. Now let's play it my way. You set up to the right, but this time, instead of hitting a fade, hitting it straight or getting a draw, you hook it. This is admittedly negative thinking, but you'll see my point in a minute. Okay, so the ball goes into the water. The difference, however, is that this time the point of entry is much closer to the target. That could make a difference in your favor of several clubs. Instead of having to play your third shot (after one-stroke penalty) with a 3-iron, from the front of the hazard, you could be taking a 5-iron from a point of entry closer to the hole.

When the trouble is on the right, you simply reverse this strategy: set up to the left and fade the ball. And again, the same thinking will give you more margin for error. Only an outright slice will put you in the hazard, and even then your point of entry will be farther up the hazard than a straight ball. If you hit a hook, a straight

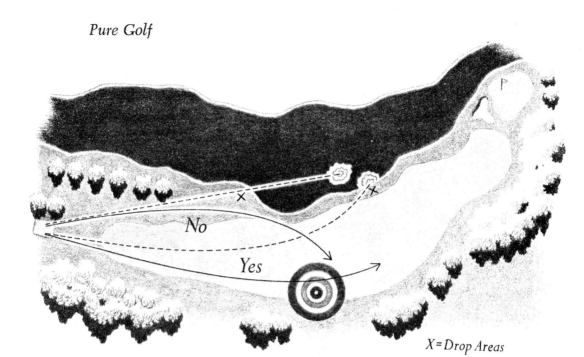

X = Drop Areas

The theory that you should aim at the trouble and bend the ball away from it leaves a lot to be desired, to my way of thinking. Say you had a water hazard on the left and you hit the ball straight. The point-of-entry rule would force you to drop the ball close to the front of the hazard. Whereas, were you to aim to the right and, at worst, snap-hook the shot, with the amount of roll your point of entry would be a lot farther forward, toward the target; also you'd have less club into the green and despite a penalty would still have a chance at recovering par.

ball, or the desired fade, you miss the hazard. Again, you have three chances out of four of missing the hazard, versus only one out of two under the old theory.

There's another reason why I dislike the idea of hitting toward a hazard and trying to curve the ball away from it, and that is this strategy can often terrorize people into making a bad swing. Even I would not be immune to it. For example, let's take the tee shot at the eighteenth hole at Pebble Beach, which has a lateral water hazard all down the left side. If I were to step on to that tee, aim ten feet left of the water hazard margin, and try to fade the ball back to the fairway, there would be a very good chance I'd say to myself, "Don't hit it straight," and, such is the power of autosuggestion, I might easily wind up hitting it straight into the water, or even miss the shot completely. Whereas my way, I get onto the tee and line up to the right.

Although I'm conscious of the trouble on the left—I wouldn't be human if I weren't—I know from experience that I can hit the ball only so far off line on a given shot. So if I'm playing away from the trouble, by the time I get over the ball, I have convinced myself that there's no way that I can hit so badly that I can go in the water. So my planned draw will come off because I have built up my confidence by playing the percentage shot.

There's another old idea about avoiding trouble from the tee that is also frequently accepted as gospel and that is: Tee up on the same side of the teeing ground as the trouble and play away from it. I don't go along with this idea, chiefly because that's not, and should never be, your top priority in selecting a place to tee the ball. When I get on a tee, I look first and foremost for a good flat spot, where I can get good traction. Whenever you think of teeing on one side or the other to avoid trouble, you can get overly scared of the trouble and could very well overcompensate in hitting away from it. Personally, I don't look at the right side or the left side of the tee; I just find a good spot and go.

In fact, locking yourself into one side or other from the tee can defeat your objectives. Why? Because tees are not necessarily flat all over. Let's take an example. Suppose the trouble is on the right side of the hole. You tee up on the right side and let's assume the ball is lower than your feet. You slice it so badly that it goes into the trouble anyway. The reason, of course, is that, when you have a sidehill lie where the ball is lower than your feet, you will have a tendency to slice. So, it would have been far better to have found a flat spot anywhere on the tee, aimed away from the trouble, and hit it straight or with just a trace of fade.

The type of shot you want to hit from the tee can also dictate where to tee the ball. Suppose you want a fade, then by all means pick a spot where the ball will be, if anything, slightly below your feet. It will help you execute the shot you want. The last thing you would want to do is to select a lie where the ball is above your feet, as this lie produces a hook.

In looking for the right spot to tee the ball, please don't forget that the teeing area is two club-lengths deep. It makes little sense to tee up on an uneven lie between the markers when by dropping back a little you can tee the ball on the most perfect lie imaginable. Another way of putting this is that so many amateurs are so distance conscious that they grudge giving up even an inch to the course. This makes no sense. You're better off giving the course a yard or two if this means you will hit the ball right on the screws.

One of the places where it makes a lot of sense to give up a yard or two is on par-3's, where if you tee up between the markers, your ball will be sitting there between dozens of divot holes. Not only can this be distracting, but the divot holes often are pointing in the wrong direction. These can influence the direction you swing through the ball and usually for the worse. If you're going to tee up between the markers, then always find a divot mark that points right at the target, and tee up behind that. It will actually help you retain a clear perspective of the target line.

As regards dog-leg holes, I think the main mistake golfers make is that they are always trying to work the ball around the dog-leg, in other words, hook around a dog-leg to the left and slice around a dog-leg to the right. The plain truth of the matter is that on most dog-leg holes you don't have to work the ball around the corner. You are far better off hitting it straight down the middle and then going into the green on your second shot.

If you analyze it, a shot straight down the middle is the per-centage shot. Say you have a dog-leg to the left. If you hit it straight down the middle, with no slice or hook, obviously you can go around the dog-leg on your second. If you hit it down the middle and hook it by accident, you'll probably go around the corner and be in fine shape. Even if you slice it a little, you will have a longer shot in but

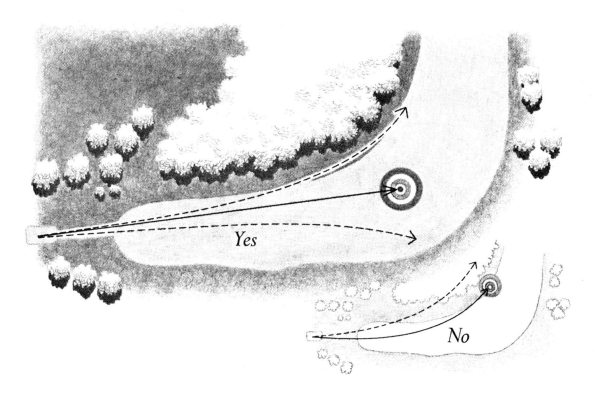

Yes

No

You'll be working against the odds by trying to play the ball close to the corner of a dog-leg. If you aim straight down the middle you can draw, hook, hit the ball straight, or fade it and not get into trouble. You have more options.

will still be safe. However, trying to play the ball close to the corner of the dog-leg gives you little chance. You have hit a perfect shot to succeed, and most of us, even us professionals, just don't hit perfect shots all the time.

About the only time I would recommend trying to work the ball around a dog-leg is, first, if you have the shot in your bag, and, second, there is a good reason for attempting the shot.

As regards having the shot in your bag, I certainly don't have to tell you how to slice if in fact you have been slicing all your life. If you are a slicer, then the dog-leg to the right is made for you. Simply play right up the middle and let your natural slice carry the ball around the corner. The same goes for the natural hooker of the ball, only this time the dog-leg to the left is your meat. Play up the middle and let the hook carry the ball around the corner.

However, if you hit the ball reasonably straight, let's review when you should consider cutting the corner of a dog-leg or working the ball around. The answer is there must be a very tangible benefit to you for taking the risk. Most of the time this means close to a ninety-degree dog-leg before it becomes worth the risk. On such a hole, cutting the corner or working it around can mean the difference between hitting a simple pitch shot into the green and hitting a 5-iron. Obviously, the wedge shot can set up a birdie for you. Against this, you have to weigh how important setting up this birdie is versus the real risk that you might leave the ball in whatever trouble—trees, rough, hazards, etc.—there is in the corner of the dog-leg. As a general rule, I would say consider it only if you're behind in a match or a tournament and have to risk everything to win, or in a four-ball match where your partner has already safely driven on the hole, or in some comparable situation.

As to how to work the ball to the left or right, I would refer you back to the shotmaking chapter where I went into this in detail. In addition to the information in that chapter, I would like to emphasize a couple of points. First, on a dog-leg to the left, I will nearly always take a 3-wood. This is because, in closing the face to get the draw or hook, you are reducing the loft to the point where you couldn't get the ball up enough with a driver. On the dog-leg to the right, you can use your driver, of course, as opening the face increases the loft. Second, how you tee the ball is most important. You may remember my telling you that when your ball was sitting down on a close lie, your general tendency would be to fade the ball and when it was sitting up high in the grass you would tend to hook. Well, when you're faced with a tee shot where you want to curve the ball, you simply apply this principle to the height you tee the ball. If you want to fade the ball, you tee it low, and when you want to hook the ball, you tee it high. Teeing it low makes you lead longer with the left

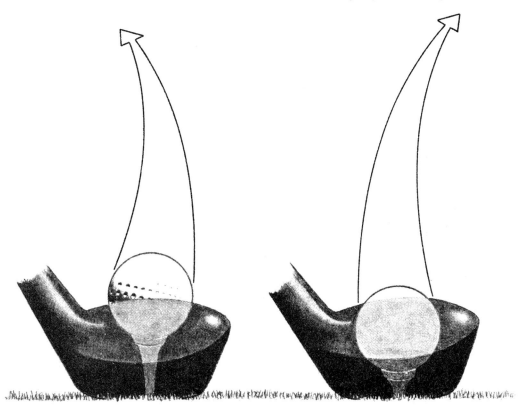

To play a draw or intentional hook, tee the ball higher. For a fade or intentional slice, tee it lower.

hand through impact, leaving the clubface open, favoring a fade, and teeing it high encourages a full release of the hands at impact, favoring a hook.

As regards tee shots generally, I map out the type of shot I want to play on each hole before I ever start my round. In practice, I'll note on a card where I'll go with an iron or fairway wood and where I can let out shaft with a driver. *The only thing I hardly ever do is break my game plan.* A lot of players do that and it's bad strategy. For example, suppose you've decided to play a 2-iron off a cer-

157

tain tee to lay up short of a mess of bunkers in the landing area. Then, suddenly you decide to go for the carry with a driver. You get over the ball and something in the back of your mind says, "I should be hitting a 2-iron, not a driver." So, you tighten up, make a bad swing, and go right into the bunkers. Once you've made up your game plan, stick to it. Again, the only exception to this would be if you have to make a change to win a tournament, or if you're so far behind in a match that you have to throw caution to the winds. Then, you have to be aggressive. But, in such a case, your mind will be at peace with your decision because circumstances have forced it on you.

In the same way that the type of shot you plan off the tee is influenced by the type of hole you're playing, so the shot into the green is governed by, first, your lie and, second, the situation at the green. I have a system that I use in evaluating these shots that I think would be dynamite for any player: I call it the "light" system.

If there's nothing to stop me hitting directly at the flag, I call this a "green light" situation. I've considered the pin placement, the trouble around the green, and all the other factors, and I have decided that there's no way I can get into trouble. The "green light" situation is purely when all systems say "Go." If there are a couple of variables against me, then I call this a "yellow light" situation. Very probably I'll play a percentage shot to the middle of the green. The "yellow light" situation is where your computer shows a couple of caution lights. Every once in a while you'll have a "red light" situation. As its name implies, this brings all normal plans to a halt. You just have to chip out of the trouble you're in the best way you can, even if it means conceding a stroke to the course.

To show you how the "light system" works out in practice, let's take a situation where I am 155 yards away from the pin and the hole is on the back of the green on the left. Right away, I know that I need a hook-spin 7-iron. My maximum for a straight shot with a 7-iron is 150 yards, but I'll get another 5 yards if I hook it a little. I look at the lie and it's perfect. I look at the trouble around the green; I can ignore the bunkers in front because the pin's at the back, and

I'll be pitching the ball in the middle of the green, and I can forget about the bunker at the back because I know I can't hit the 7-iron more than 155 yards, even with a hook. Since there's nothing to prevent me shooting right at the pin, that's a "green light" situation.

Now let's assume the same general circumstances with these changes: the green is very shallow, the pin is tucked left with bunkers at the front on the left and at the back of the green, and to top it off I have a skinny, tight lie. This lie favors a fade, not a hook, and this factor, added to the tough pin placement, means I've got several factors against me. So, it's a "yellow light" situation and I would play a percentage shot for the fat part of the green.

Third, let's assume that the shot is being played from the left rough. The lie is heavy and I've got to go under a tree to hit toward the green. If I punch a little 5-iron under and out, then I won't have enough loft on the ball to carry the bunker on the left and stop the ball on the green. If I play for the opening of the green, the ball could very well run through the green into the bunker on the right. Whichever way I look at it, I'm dead! This is strictly a "red light" situation. What I'd do is just punch the ball out short of the green and hope for a pitch and putt to save par. (Illustrations follow page 160.)

There's one additional point that's worth making about this "red light" situation. Just because you're "dead" in the sense that you can't attempt to hit the green doesn't mean you should just punch it out anywhere. Take the time to figure out the place from which it will be the easiest to get it up and down for your par, and try to hit the ball to that point. You should always try to set up your next shot—even from "red light" situations—if at all possible.

You can see, then, that my "light system" can readily be applied to your own game. It's just a matter of understanding your game and knowing your own capabilities. If, for example, you have a tendency to hit the ball reasonably straight but low all the time, and you're playing a course with a lot of elevated greens, then you're going to be playing a lot of "yellow light" golf that day. You're obviously not going to be able to go for a flag that is tucked behind a bunker because you don't have the height. You'll have to take one or two more clubs to clear the trouble. The main thing is to know your pluses and minuses when you're plotting your strategy and to always play your strongest suit.

Another vital element in deciding whether a situation is "green," "yellow," or "red" is how you are playing. If you're playing badly, then perhaps there will never be a "green light" that day. You'll just have to play on yellow all the time. However, "yellow light" golf isn't necessarily bad golf—I've played eighteen holes of "yellow light" golf and shot 68. Another time you might get too cocky and play "green light" golf all the way around and shoot a bad round. But this is all part of experience. In my own game, I have learned the difference between how I'm hitting at the time and the variables that affect each shot. You, too, will have to learn that for yourself.

The type of shot you should consider playing into any specific green is first and foremost a product of your lie. If your lie is bad, then you should go ahead and play a percentage shot to the opening of the green. However, assuming your lie is good, then the shot you play should be influenced by conditions at the green.

Obviously, if the pin placement is right in the opening to the green, you have no problem. You can play right at it. But what if the pin is tucked left or right behind a bunker? The answer here depends on your ability. If you have just one shot in your bag and that's more or less of a straight ball, then you should definitely play for the fat part of the green and let your putter do the talking for you. But if you can move the ball both ways, then this is where your shotmaking ability can really pay off.

What you do is hit the center of the green and then work toward the hole with the appropriate spin. If the pin is tucked right, then you would put slice-spin on the ball, and if it's tucked left, hook-spin. When playing these shots, remember the characteristics of these spins as regards selecting a landing area. On a slice-spin shot, when the ball lands, it takes a "straight up" bounce and then sucks right. So your landing area should only be a few yards short of the pin as regards distance. But on a hook-spin shot, the ball will

I consider the twelfth hole at Augusta National (Par 3, 155 yards) a "red light" situation. When the pin is tucked in the sliver of green on the left midway between the front and back bunkers, there is always danger. Especially in pressure situations, I'll play out to the right of the green.

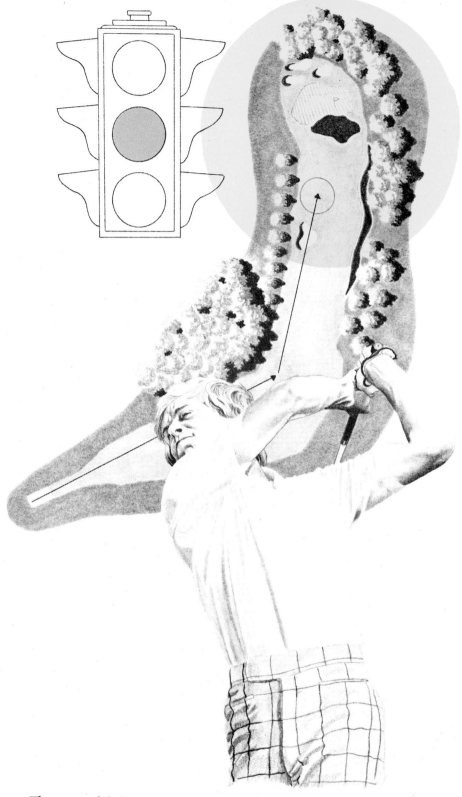

The sixteenth hole at Firestone Country Club, in Akron, Ohio, where I won the World Series in 1974, could be described as a "yellow light" situation. You must use extreme caution. It's a reachable par-5 with two long wood shots (625 yards), but should your second shot stray to the right, it will catch the water. If there is ever any doubt in my mind on this hole, I'll always take an iron, play short, and then pitch in to the flag.

The seventeenth hole at Oakhill is a "green light" hole. Although it's a good par-4 463-yard hole, it's reachable and doesn't offer serious trouble. At worst, I may hit into a greenside bunker, which would mean I still have a chance at par.

The pin placement must always dictate the type of shot you opt to play. In other words, if the pin is tucked left, play a draw. If the pin is to the right, play a fade.

take a long sliding skid type of bounce and then roll a lot more, so the landing area should be well short of the pin to allow for this action.

Working the ball into the pin is really the ideal way to play to tucked pins because you're combining the best of both worlds—a percentage shot to the fat part of the green, plus an attacking shot in the sense that you're kicking the ball toward the pin to leave yourself a shorter putt. Firing straight at the pin doesn't make much sense unless you're playing so well you just know you can make the shot.

When I'm playing well, I'm programming everything into my mind—not only the slope in the landing area, which is a fairly obvious thing to do, but the grain of the grass as well. For example, if I know that the grain is going dead right and the flag is also on the right, then I can play to the center of the green with a cut shot, put left-to-right spin on the ball, and know that it's going to hit and go right farther than usual. Conversely, if the grain runs to the left and the pin is tucked left, the ball will run left more than normal. If the grain is against the kick of the spin, then I know that either I'll have to land the ball closer to the pin initially or be satisfied with a longer putt if it's safer to land the ball in the middle of the green.

If the grain on the green runs away from me and I play a reasonably straight sort of shot, then I'm assured that the ball will take a long bounce and roll a lot more than usual. And if it's against me, then I know the ball will take more of a straight-up bounce and stop quickly. These are things that a lot of players don't program, but, if they did, they would be better players.

If some greens have big breaks or heavy undulations, I always mark that down on the card in practice, so when I'm doing my preshot programming, I'll take into consideration the type of putt I want to leave myself. This goes double if you're playing really fast greens, like U. S. Open Greens, where being just anywhere on the green doesn't guarantee you're in two-putt range. For example, if the pin is in the middle of a green that slopes severely from front to back, then the last thing I'd want to do is to carry the ball past the flag. I would think instead of a club that would leave me below the hole for certain. Or, if the flag is just left of center on a green that sloped from left to right, I certainly wouldn't play a draw shot in that case, because conceivably the ball could roll up above the flag, leaving me a downhill putt. I'd fade the shot to make certain of an uphill putt from the right of the flag. Conversely, if the pin is right of center on a right-to-left slope, I draw the ball to leave it below the flag on the left.

If the green slopes down from back to front, a punch shot will produce the best results because of its low trajectory. This is also a good shot into the back level of a double-tiered green. If you can also put a little hook-spin on the ball, so much the better. I find that, because of the long skip and roll, this type of shot is the best to combat the hill going up to the second tier. One thing is for sure: If the pin is back on the top level, you surely don't want to hit a high spot. If it bounces on the top level, it can barrel right on through the green, and if it pitches into the slope between the tiers, it will roll down to the bottom level, leaving you staring at a three-putt situation.

Elevated greens are the trickiest to gauge correctly. I've found that a high "floater" works best here. The floater is also useful when the pin is tucked behind a bunker in the front of the green, and you really want to get the ball close.

Select the Clubs to Suit Conditions

Strategy, to my way of thinking, includes choosing the correct clubs to use on any particular round. Your selection will be based on such elements as the type of shots needed on the course, severity of the rough, weather, etc. I know this philosophy probably sounds a little strange to you because, in all probability, you have fourteen clubs in your bag, and the rules only allow fourteen, right?

That's exactly right, but my point is that all golfers—not just professionals—could benefit by owning a couple of extra clubs, then selecting the best fourteen to get the job done on the round at hand.

In my own case, I normally carry a driver, 3-wood, and 4-wood, 2–9 in the irons, pitching wedge, sand wedge, and putter, and the only club I will leave out of my bag will be the 4-wood to make room for either a 5-wood or a 1-iron. Here are some examples of when and why I will pick one of these three over the others.

If I'm playing in the British Open, I normally use the 1-iron if the course is dry and there's a lot of roll on the ball. This is because over there your first consideration has to be the rough, which is knee-high and takes a wedge to get out of most of the time. The 1-iron is a great club for me in such a situation because I can rely on hitting it straight up to about 230 yards. Sometimes more. And if I do go into the rough, the 4-wood or even the 5-wood won't be of much use 90 per cent of the time.

If the course is wet, as it often is at the Crosby, then I'll go with the 5-wood. Long irons—and especially the 1-iron—become difficult to use in the wet, and I find I can rely on the 5-wood to get the ball up in the air for me. I also play a lot of choked 5-woods to substitute for some long iron shots if the lie is bad.

I know that a lot of amateurs think that using a 5-wood is a kind of copout. Bunk! It's a great club not only in the wet but also out of heavy rough. I won the 1974 Tournament of Champions because I carried a 5-wood. The rough was very heavy and most of the time a 4-wood wouldn't have done the job. But my little 5-wood got the ball up and out of there easy as you please.

When I play in Florida, I'll generally leave the 1-iron and the 5-wood out of the bag and carry my 4-wood. The reasoning here is the rough isn't quite as long as, say, in the East, and you get more lies where the ball sits up. Because of these elements, I know that I can use the 4-wood to my advantage.

In your own case, assuming you carry the same normal set as I do, you should certainly think of making room in your bag for a 5-wood when the conditions or weather dictates it. If it's wet, for example, you could consider leaving out your 2-iron, which will be as useless to you as my 1-iron would be to me, and substituting a 5-wood. If it's windy, you might reverse the thinking—drop the 5-wood and play the 2-iron. Then, suppose the course you're going to play has a lot of elevated greens, and let's assume you normally would have to hit a lot of long irons in there. Drop the 2-iron and use the 5-wood again. If necessary, choke down on the 5-wood for some shots that would otherwise demand a 3- or 4-iron. Of course,

I'm assuming here that you have difficulty hitting high long irons, but I think it's a good assumption for all but low-handicappers.

Now I've said that I personally interchange only the 4-wood, 5-wood, and 1-iron, but that's no reason why you shouldn't make up any set of fourteen clubs that will do the job for you. Remember, I'm just doing what's best for me—you should do the same for yourself. For example, you might want to play driver, 3-, 4-, and 5-woods and drop the 2-iron, or keep the 2-iron and use a utility wedge instead of a pitching wedge and sand wedge. Or you might even want to make room in your bag for a chipper. I've seen some amateurs who are excellent with a chipper, even when they don't hit many other clubs in their bag very well. Of course the reason for their skill with this club is that they play it all the time, and so they really get to know it well.

The point of all this really is that I think that average players don't choose clubs to play a specific round with. They just go out with what they have. The reason for this is not hard to find. When they buy a new set of clubs, they lock themselves into a certain selection of clubs by just buying thirteen clubs, assuming they already have a putter. To my way of thinking, it would be far better if they bought all the clubs they could conceivably use even if this number did run the total number above fourteen. They would then be in a position to make an intelligent selection before each round.

In fact, having more than fourteen clubs would force them to select the best clubs before every round—otherwise they would be breaking the rules of golf and be penalized for the extra club. This would be just great, in my opinion. Remember, we professionals select clubs in this way all the time. You should do so too. If it only saves you a couple of strokes a round, it will have been well worth the investment.

PLAYING IN THE WIND AND WET AND COLD

I'm probably fortunate to have grown up in San Francisco because our climate varies so much. As a kid I played in my share of wet weather in tournaments in that area. Also, in playing along the coast, down in Monterey especially, I learned—I should say, had to learn—how to cope with the wind. I think that's one reason why I generally play quite well in Britain. I know not only how to keep the ball down, but also how to cope with rain and the cold.

One of these years I'm going to put it all together over there. That would be great. It would be the first time a Californian would take home that old "pot" as the British affectionately call trophies, since one of my boyhood idols, Tony Lema, won it in 1966.

To return to our subjects, let's deal first with wind, then wet weather, and then how to beat the cold. Although nobody likes them, there will be days when you'll just have to live with them.

On windy days, there's no doubt that playing into the wind gives the average golfer the most problems. He just can't keep the ball down. The reason for this is that he makes the mistake of swinging harder to compensate for the force of the wind. Now when you do that the extra force in your swing and the action of the wind will put additional backspin on the ball, and the next thing you know is that you've "ballooned" the ball up into the air.

The key to successful play into the wind is to put as *little* spin on the ball as possible, and you do that by slowing your swing down. I've found that with a slow swing the ball doesn't climb up the face of the club so much and, consequently, doesn't produce as much backspin. You hit a semisoft shot that bores right through the wind like an arrow. To compensate for the softer swing and the force of the wind, you should use one or two clubs stronger than normal.

I think you will find the RPM gauge image I referred to earlier in the book useful in this situation. If your red line is 7,000 RPM, drop back to 6,500 into the wind and you'll handle these difficult shots with more authority.

Downwind off the tee, the great tendency is to get greedy and try to hit the ball a country mile. Somehow the knowledge that the wind should give you extra distance is enough to make most golfers emulate a contestant in a long driving contest. That's *bad* thinking, or perhaps I should say a complete absence of thinking. It's true that you should get more distance downwind, but only if you meet the ball solidly, and this means swinging normally. Another point that is useful off the tee is to take a more lofted club than normal because the wind will take some backspin off the ball and it will not climb as readily as on a still day. Instead of taking a driver, tee it up with a 3-wood, hit it solid, and you'll get a good trajectory to the shot, which will go farther than your normal driver shot.

Playing into the green, you're going to have to allow for the wind by taking less club than normal. But don't make the mistake of just tossing the ball up into the air and leaving it at the mercy of the wind. I learned this point while playing with Jack Nicklaus. I noticed that any approach shot that he had downwind was punched low. The only exception was if he needed a high shot to clear a bunker or some other form of trouble in front of the green. The main objection to the high shot downwind is that it is practically impossible to predict how far the ball will travel. Once it's up in the air, the wind can blow harder, which will send it farther, or die and you'll come up short. It's also tough to predict how much spin you're going to get on the ball for the same reasons. This is what makes the punch shot, with its lower trajectory, the percentage shot; whatever the wind does, you'll get somewhere on the green and certainly a whole lot closer than just hitting it up in the air and saying a prayer.

When it comes to crosswinds, a lot of players say you should hold the ball into the wind by drawing the ball into a left-to-right wind and cutting it into a right-to-left wind. I disagree with that thinking and here's why. For example, if you're going to draw the ball into a left-to-right wind, you have to set up to the right of the hole. Suppose that hook doesn't come off and you hit it straight. Not only have you hit it to the right of the pin, but the wind will carry it farther to the right. The same thing applies in reverse to cutting the ball into a right-to-left wind. You could have the ball flying left to left.

Instead, I recommend that in a left-to-right wind you set up to the left of the pin and fade the ball or at least set up left and attempt to hit a straight ball and let the ball drift to the right toward the pin. Even if you drew the ball a little by mistake, the wind would tend to straighten out its flight, and you wouldn't be as far off line to the left as you would be to the right with the other method. Conversely, in a right-to-left wind, I recommend that you set up to the right of the flag and either draw it in or hit a straight ball to the right, which will come back to the pin with the wind.

When it comes to wet weather play, the first thing to remember is that, as I said earlier, the long irons become very difficult to use. Go with your 5-wood whenever possible even to the point of choking down on it to avoid playing a long iron. The 5-wood will give a high, dropping shot that will at least sit down in a reasonably predictable way.

In most cases, you can rely on the ball traveling at least one club farther in wet weather. The reason for this is that water gets between the grooves on the club and the ball, so the ball sort of shoots off the clubface with little backspin. The exception to this is if the rain is falling while you're playing—then you have to expect to lose a little distance due to the resistance to the ball's flight set up by the falling raindrops.

In the short game, don't try and chip the ball with a 5- or 7-iron if that is what you normally do. You'll find it very difficult if not impossible to predict how the ball will react on landing. In this case, take a leaf from my book and use your wedges—you'll find that the "all air" route is much easier. When putting, the cardinal rule is—don't be short! The ball is going to encounter a lot of resistance from the water along the route, and you've got to convince yourself to hit the ball harder than usual. Even if you hit the ball a little too hard, it's going to slow down a lot faster than usual, so you have a lot more margin for error. Lastly, remember that you don't get as much break on a wet green—if the ground is really wet, you can cut the normal break in half.

Cold weather is always a problem, even to the best players. When it's cold, you tend to lose that all-important "feel" in the hands. You find that your range of motion shortens because your muscles tighten. You also find that a cold golf ball doesn't compress as easily and as a result you can't hit it as far.

The first thing to do to combat the conditions is to be sure you're well dressed. I wear thermal underwear, wool slacks, a turtleneck sweater, a short-sleeve sweater, and a long-sleeve sweater over the top. In very cold weather I'll carry a hand warmer to maintain as much feel as I can in my hands. If you don't have a hand warmer, stick your hands in your pockets or wear a warm, lined pair of winter gloves between shots. As regards combating the problem of cold golf balls, I find it best to rotate three balls, using a new ball on each tee, and keeping the other two in a pocket to stay warm. If it's really cold, use a slightly lower-compression ball than usual; if you use a 90 compression normally, drop back to 80 or so. The problem with the high-compression balls in the cold is that they get as hard as rocks—you'll find the lower-compression ball much more comfortable to hit.

Earlier in this book, I went on record as being against practice swings as well. Well, cold weather is the one exception to this general rule. Your muscles will tend to get tight between shots so that the only way you can get the blood flowing and extend your range of motion is to take a couple of practice swings.

PLAY THE PERCENTAGES

If I had to sum up this whole chapter in one phrase, it would have to be—play the percentages. The problem with the average golfer is that he tends to remember only the good shots he occasionally hits rather than the bad ones. So, when he's faced with a particular situation, he doesn't think, "Well, I can only make this shot three times out of ten, but the other shot I can make nine times out of ten," and then go with the safer shot. He just remembers the few times he played the more dangerous shot perfectly.

Ninety-shooters remain 90-shooters because they think, "This is the situation, and I have to do it now," instead of trying to play a smart shot, a shot they have a good chance of pulling off. You'll see guys shooting with a wood to a tiny green built to hold a short-iron second. Why? Because they missed their drive on this short par-4, they feel they have to get on with their second. Bunk! If *I* had to shoot at that green with a 3-wood, I couldn't hold it. Instead, they should be thinking of laying up short and then pitching to save par.

Don't put each shot in a "one ball" perspective. Think of it in a ten-ball or even better a twenty-five-ball perspective. Believe me, the shot you should play is not the one you make only once in twenty-five attempts, but the one you might *miss* only one time in twenty-five. If you can picture that, you're always going to play great percentage golf.

CHAPTER ELEVEN

Programming Your Mental Computer

I believe that our potential in golf, or any other endeavor for that matter, is not even close to being fulfilled. Why? Because, until recent years, the only improvements that have been made in playing the game have been on the physical side. Yet in the physical area we have proven that a lot of people can get the job done even though they have a lousy swing and don't hit a lot of good shots. However, they are effective in other areas. They're smart, they have good programming, they think out their swings, map out their shots and the course well, and, above all, believe in their own ability. Yes, it's on the mental side that the big improvements in the game will be made. To me, properly programmed golf is "pure" golf, golf as it should be played.

You must remember that your golf swing will always be basically what it was when you first developed it in the early stages of your golf. Even after refining it and changing bits and pieces of it, if a guy hasn't seen you in ten years, since your amateur days, he could spot your swing from three fairways over. Sometimes, I suppose you might see someone that's really changed his swing, but I can't think of anyone personally.

Many people make mental changes, however. And that's the difference really between winners and nonwinners; proper attitude, believing in yourself, and going the extra mile as far as creative thinking goes.

Most people aren't creative at all, either in learning the physical side of the game or the mental. As regards the mechanics of the swing, they just read an article in a golf magazine or buy the latest book on golf and then try to emulate *everything* they read. They're copycats with the blinders on who never stop to think whether this "latest thing" is suitable for them as individuals. You've got to remember that everybody's different—both as regards physique and mentality—so that it follows that every teaching method will be as different as the individual expounding it. That's the whole thing in golf, the individuality of the game. There is no one swing that you can copy, and no one method that works for everybody. You have to find out what works for you and then try to understand the key ingredients of your own method.

Even I, after several years on the tour, still have a long way to go with learning what's good for me. But at least I'm aware of the problem. So many players aren't aware. They know you've got to be positive and think you're going to make it, but they don't go about trying to understand the problem in a very professional way.

I look at it this way. Your mind is a computer and your body just works off the data that is stored in your brain. So, for example, if you develop a clear and concise way of hitting a golf ball, you can literally become like a machine. The swing can become so ingrained that you don't forget it. It becomes as automatic as touch-typing or tying your shoes. It's the same way with your planning. The great thinkers have a sheet of paper in front of them, and they map their whole day out. Their minds are always thinking ahead. They know the next hole, the next shot and are ready for them.

Just about everything we do involves programming our mental computer. Suppose you're giving a speech. Hopefully, you've programmed it before you get up on your feet. If you have made notes beforehand of the key ideas you want to put across, and have put them down in a logical order, then your speech should be fine. If not, your speech won't be very good. The same thing applies to a business executive first thing in the morning. He or she will sit down, make a list of the things to be done, place them in order of priority, and then follow through in that order.

I could go on, but the point is that successful golf is precisely the same—the more good key ideas and thoughts you program into your brain, the better you are going to play.

But how do you do that? How do you program your mental computer? By a process commonly called visualization. Although that's a six-syllable word, don't be frightened of it. All it means is to see something in your mind or to make a mental image of it. You do it all the time, if you stop to think about it.

For example, take our example of the speech. When you list your key thoughts, you have a mental image of yourself speaking the words you want to say. When you organize the ideas into the proper order, you visualize several ways in which you can present your ideas, then pick the best way after reviewing the mental images of each in your mind. Then, when you make the speech, just looking at each point on your list brings the appropriate mental image to your mind and you find yourself saying the words exactly as you had visualized them in advance.

Golf is exactly the same. The only way you can program your mental computer is by means of visual images. And this applies whether you're working on your swing, learning to hit different shots, planning your round, or programming individual shots—whatever you're trying to do in golf at a particular point in time.

Visualization and Your Swing

When you first start off in golf, you have literally no visual image of how to execute the golf swing. So, the only thing to do is pick out model golf swings and try to emulate them. When I started off, my dad showed me pictures of Hogan and Snead, and even today you couldn't get better models. However, of the current tour stars I would certainly recommend two for particular study—Al Geiberger and Tom Weiskopf.

Al's swing looks upright because he's tall, but in reality he takes it back on the line in a perfect plane. Tom's swing is also just about as good as any I've seen. It's a good solid swing—compact, powerful, and effortless. To me that's the kind of swing to have—one where you don't have to work 100 per cent to get the ball out there for good distance. Both Al and Tom have excellent balance, keeping themselves perfectly centered over the ball. There are not many people who do that.

You should use every chance you get to formulate good mental images of the swing. Watch your professional, watch the really low handicap players at your course, study sequence pictures of great players in books and magazines, and study the swings of the best players on TV. Compare some of the best players with some of the less talented players on the tour. A particularly good time to learn is when the tour hits your area. Go to the practice tee and look down the line of players practicing. Slowly, you will learn to pick out what the great players do that the lesser don't. All of this sharpens your perceptions of the swing and makes for sharp, clear mental images for your own use.

Little by little you'll compile a list of fundamentals of your own swing; these are the mental images that get the job done for you. However, at this point in your career, you will find that much of what you have learned is ingrained—it's in your subconscious. Because of this, changes in your swing do become more difficult. For example, if you have been swinging a certain way for three years and all of a sudden change and offer your subconscious a new method of swinging, be prepared to spend considerable time working on it. Major change cannot be made overnight.

However, don't make the mistake of thinking you're stuck then with what you've got. There are many people like that. Tell them to make a correction in their backswing, and they'll take it back the same way they always have, no matter how many times they swing. In other words, they're like muscle morons. The reason why they're like that, in my opinion, is that they don't make use of mental images. In fact, they probably don't have any clear idea of how they swing at all. So, how can they modify the unknown? I was always the opposite of this—I could always change my swing. And the reason I could was my early training in the game with Dad. I started formulating my swing by means of mental images, which have become sharpened and clarified over the years. Even though you may not have made conscious use of mental images before, I assure you that visualization is improvable and the only way to perfect your swing.

There is one caution here: If you have an established swing, don't try to feed too many conscious images into your subconscious mind at once. It just won't work. You'll just give your subconscious a case of indigestion. Feed new images in one at a time preferably, and certainly no more than two.

Lastly, I would like to reiterate what I said earlier in this book. Mental pictures are the way you program your subconscious, but no amount of visualization is any good if the mental pictures used aren't accurate. Make use of every visual aid you can lay your hands on, be it a full-length mirror, still pictures and movies of your swing, or TV replay machines. In this way, you will be able to "see" your swing honestly at all times.

Visualization and Individual Shots

You should look at every shot just as if you were programming a computer. You have to become machine-like in your mental preparation just as much as in the physical. Earlier in this book I described my physical pattern of taking address, the actions I go through from the time I take the club out of my bag until I draw the club back. Now, we're going to put that together with proper preshot thinking.

In actual fact, you can't separate the two. They work together. To really become as machine-like as possible, you have to go through the same physical procedure every time at address, whether you're playing for two cents or the Open. This is so that when you are under pressure your setup is not something you have to think about. You just become mechanized. You'll never see Arnold Palmer or Jack Nicklaus ever just sloppily walk up and hit the ball without going through their own pattern, and neither should you. You've got to take the same amount of looks at the hole, repeat the same procedure over and over again regardless of the situation.

Not only does a standardized pattern of taking address take care of the routine mechanics of getting into the proper physical position—ball position, alignment, etc.—but it's also a discipline for the mind, to keep your thoughts going right down the track without any undesirable side trips. Another plus factor of a set pattern is that it gives you the time to form the correct mental images before playing the shot.

Average players don't set up to the ball in an orderly fashion. They just want to pull a club out of the bag and let it fly, without thinking. That's why they remain 100 shooters. I really believe that the reason I've done as well as I have in recent years is that, in the same way an airplane pilot has a checklist and runs through it prior to takeoff, I have a mental checklist that I run through before every shot.

How would the checklist read? Well, the first thing on it is what kind of a lie you've got. The lie always affects the way you

MY PRESHOT CHECKLIST. 1. The type of lie I have. 2. Where the trouble is. 3. The wind direction and yardage. 4. Position of the flag. 5. The way the green slopes. 6. The way I'm swinging.

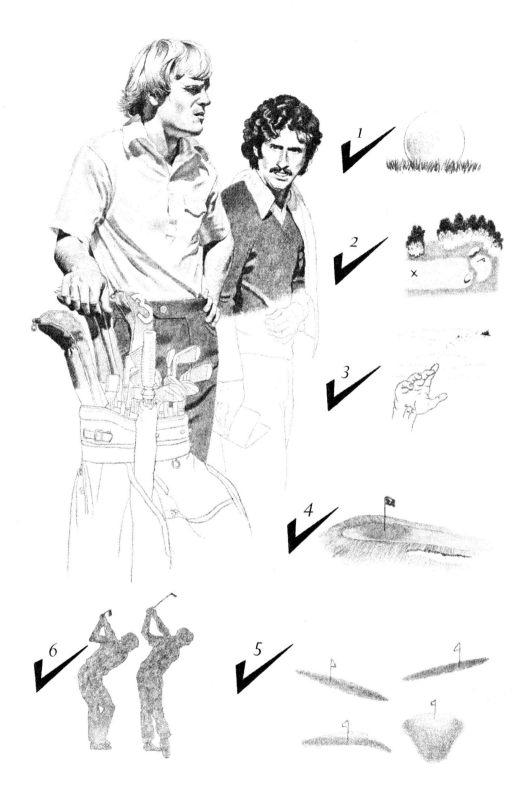

stand to the ball. In other words, you have all these shots in your bag, but the lie may eliminate all but two or three of them. Then, of course, you must know the yardage, wind or weather conditions and their effect, the situation at the target or green area including pin position, hazards, how hard the green is, relevant slopes on the green and grain. You figure out what your strongest shot is. By now you've got a lot of confidence because you know the shot you're playing is the right one. Then you go ahead and visualize your swing and how the shot is going to fly and land. Then you go ahead and hit it. That covers just about everything except that on the putting green, of course, you are visualizing the ball rolling along the line to the hole, rather than through the air.

However, it's not enough to just go through such a checklist in a mechanical way. You've got to employ mental images all the way—visualize everything, in fact. For example, when you look at the lie you visualize the types of shot that you could play off it. See them hit, see them go off, and be honest about it. If the lie is less than perfect, you might not like what you visualize, but this is the best way to arrive at the percentage shot. The same thing with the yardage. That's just a starting point. You've got to visualize the effect of the wind and weather and the factors in the target area. Hit some more mental shots and visualize their effects.

Once you've decided the shot you want to hit, then you should visualize just how such a swing feels. I go ahead and take the swing in my mind. In effect, I'm retrieving an image of that swing from the memory of my computer, the subconscious, and I'm doing it through evoking the right mental image. The mental image retrieved is as complete as I can make it; the swing itself, how it feels hitting the ball, how the ball flies and lands up by the hole. I see the ball from the moment it leaves the club, I see its trajectory, the bounce, the roll, everything.

With proper programming, you get the right read-out and there will be no end to your progression. You can get back out only what you feed in.

Having done all this programming, I just get behind the ball maybe four or five steps and look down the line. Then, I walk up that line with maybe another picture of how that swing is going to feel, settle into my stance, take my four waggles, and pull the trigger.

If I'm hitting the ball well, I don't think of programming physical keys. I'm not thinking of keeping my head still. I'm not thinking of any of those sorts of things. It's all visual images of the swing, a solid hit, and the ball flying to the target. That's true 99 per cent of the time. But if I'm hitting the ball badly, I have to take some steps to correct it, even out on the golf course. Say, I have my hands a little too far behind the ball or I'm swaying. What I'll do is interject the correction as part of my total mental picture of the swing I want to make. If my hands are in the wrong position at address, I simply visualize myself having the hands in the correct position before imagining the picture of the swing. If the error is in the swing, then I make certain that my visual image of that portion of the swing is good and sharp.

As regards programming different types of shots, I'll sometimes visualize some other player's whole swing or I'll use bits and pieces of it. For example, you may remember I said when I want to hook the ball, I just visualize Tony Lema's swing; when I want to fade the ball, I visualize Lee Trevino's swing; and when I want to hit the ball straight, I visualize my own swing. These are examples of "whole swing" visualizations. When it comes to other shots, I'll sometimes just visualize a player's setup or something he does in his swing. For example, I'll take a little piece of Casper, who's a great chipper, or something from Chi Chi Rodriguez, who is in my opinion the best sand player of them all.

Anyway, the point is to train yourself to observe other players and always be looking for visual images that you can use in your own game. When you've found an image that can be useful to you, make a note of it so that you can retrieve it whenever you wish.

One of the most important aspects of organizing your preshot thinking along the lines I've described here is that you'll find that your concentration improves the more you do it. If you're as machine-like as possible physically, there isn't much time for negative thoughts to intrude as when you take too much time over the ball. And when you program yourself to just visualize the shot at hand, there's no room in your mind for negative images. You remember the expression: Nature abhors a vacuum. Well, your mind is rather like that vacuum. If it's empty, all sorts of mental images can rush in to fill it, and as often as not, they're undesirable ones. But fill it with positive images of what you want to do on the shot at hand, and those negative images are kept out.

To give you a target to shoot at, I remember one time playing with Gary Player at Doral. All day long I hit my own shot inside his. As we were walking up the eighteenth hole, I was waiting for Gary to say something to me, maybe compliment me on my fine play. He turned to me finally and said, "You know, this is probably the best I've ever hit the ball from tee to green." He had been concentrating so hard on his own game, he hadn't noticed a thing I was doing!

VISUALIZATION AND PLANNING YOUR ROUND

While I went rather thoroughly into the nuts and bolts of planning your strategy, what I want to stress here is the full use of mental images in such planning. You should not only plan where you want to hit the ball on the various holes, but also literally "see" in your mind an image of yourself making the shots needed. See yourself curving the ball off the tee on this hole to prevent it running down into the rough, or laying up short of bunkers that can catch a tee shot, and so on. The more vividly you can play the round ahead of time in your mind, the better you are going to play. It's like taking a test at college. The more you study, the better you are going to do.

The other aspect to preparing for a round involves preprogramming your basics on the swing and the various shots. If you have followed me so far, you should have developed lists of mental images covering every aspect of your game. You should go over these mental keys before a round.

To explain this, I would like to digress for just a moment to tell you that this is what I do when I come back to the game after a layoff. When I haven't played for a time, all I have to do is go over my swing keys for playing various shots, etc., and if I carefully reprogram these thoughts, I play as though I had been playing every day. Sometimes, I can lay off for as much as two weeks, and if I give my subconscious a quick refresher course on my basics, I have the same good feeling in my hands as if I hadn't missed a day of practice.

This may sound strange to you, but I think the key here is that you will do better after a layoff if you know your swing really well. If you don't know your swing, you had better play all the time.

A layoff for me as a professional may very well be a normal interval between rounds for you as an amateur. After all, most amateurs play only on weekends, so there's a five-day interval between rounds. In effect, you have a five-day layoff every week. If I as a professional find these mental image refresher courses invaluable after a layoff, I am sure that if you build up clear mental images of your swing and other aspects of playing the game, keep lists of them handy for reference, and replay them between weekends, you are going to find that your progression in the game is much faster.

Of course, none of this is going to be much good to you if you don't keep lists as I am suggesting. I would really urge you to make the list-making a habit. How many times have you found yourself playing badly and you thought to yourself, "Well, last month I was hitting the ball really well—what was I doing then that I'm not doing now?" If you can pull out that list, many times you can say, "Hey, here it is," and start hitting the ball well again. But if you don't have the list . . . Well, I'll let you elaborate on that!

VISUALIZATION AND YOUR OVER-ALL GAME

There's no doubt in my mind that, to a large extent, what you visualize is going to happen does happen. For example, I always seem to play well overseas. The people over there make a big deal out of me and make me feel like a big shot. As a result, I say to myself, "I'm supposed to win," and I do win—or at least come very close.

Another perfect example of that is Arnold Palmer. In 1975 he hadn't won all year in the States, but he went to Europe and won twice—the Spanish Open and the British PGA Championship. Arnold undoubtedly got all charged up over there because everyone expected him to win. And so the only image in his mind was winning. This just left no room for self-doubts in his mind.

The converse is true of foreign players who come to the U.S. Nobody makes a fuss about them here, so they get to thinking, "Well, maybe I'm not as good as the Americans." Now many of them are, but because they don't believe they are they aren't.

Anyway, the point is that to a great extent you are what you think you are. But to understand that, I think you have to interpret that thought by saying you are what you program yourself to be, and you program yourself, of course, by your own mental images.

That's why I'm not one of those guys that go over their mistakes continually. I try to recognize mistakes, learn from them so I don't make them again, but I don't try to accentuate them. I always try to accentuate the good things—how the good swings felt, and what transpired to make them good shots. That's how you improve.

To appreciate the power of positive visualization, I think you only have to look at what negative visualization can and does do to you. For example, if you ever say to yourself, "Gee, I wonder when the last time I three-putted was," I will take a bet that you'll three-putt on the next green or the green after. And you might have gone four hundred holes without taking a three-putt green! Or another example is the old bet that a guy will make with even a good golfer, namely that he can't play eighteen holes without making a double bogey. That's a super bet—that's one I wouldn't take myself. What happens is all of a sudden a bogey is a good score, because if you make bogeys, you're still winning the bet. But the trick is you set your sights so low that pretty soon you have to make a double bogey.

I'm sure that just about everything is a case of mind over matter. You can't tell yourself you're tired, or you will be. Or you get guys who will come into a tournament and say, "Man, this course is crummy! They've got lousy tees and the greens are terrible," and they program all these negative images. They are just defeating themselves. I come to a course and I try to find all the *nice* things I can about it. I tell people how good the course is and keep on telling myself the same thing. You've got to tell yourself that the accommodations are great, the food is great, the course is great; it's all part of the positive programming.

It's really incredible how powerful this visualization business is as far as programming your physical results. My eyes are opening up more and more to this all the time, perhaps more than anybody else on the tour. Maybe that's why my play is as close to that of Nicklaus or any of the other top players. I really believe that's one of the reasons I'm doing as well as I am. I realize how important it is to program the right thoughts. You must eliminate the negatives. Maybe they'll come into your mind, but you have to reason with them and say No, that's not really the problem because I'm going to do this and this and this and not that.

For example, if I catch myself saying, "Well, I'm not putting very well," if I keep on saying that I'm going to keep on putting badly. So I've got to reprogram all my basic keys on putting. I have to say to myself, "To putt well, I've got to keep the top of the handle on the level, I've got to aim the clubface at the target, I've got to keep my head still, I've got to think of the tempo on the stroke—One . . . Two, just like a pendulum," and so on. If I continually tell myself that this is what I want to accomplish in my stroke, and I know that these mental images have worked in the past, then I know that

I'll putt sensationally again. It might take a few days for the images to sink in again, but very soon I'm putting super again.

Actually, having the patience to keep on programming the positive when things are not going your way is one of the most important attributes of a golfer. I learned this from Jack Nicklaus. I talked to his caddie, Angie, one time at the '73 World Series. Jokingly, I said to him, "Angie, you must do something for Jack. He pays you a lot of money, yet, you don't do yardage, you don't do anything that I can see. What does Jack tell you to do?" His reply was very interesting. He said, "The only thing he tells me is, if things aren't going too well, just tell him to be patient."

I got to thinking about that and asked myself, "Now, why would a guy want his caddie to tell him that? He knows he's the best, right?" But Jack just wants to be reminded he's got seventy-two holes to catch up. If he's just patient and waits the bad period out, he's going to get his licks in before the tournament is over.

You see that so many times with Jack. He can be totally out of it going into the last round, and then he'll have a good last round and win the whole thing.

This thinking has really helped me. A lot of times I'll go out and I'll get three over par after four holes. But I know from experience that, before that eighteenth hole comes around, I'm going to get my licks in. If I just let it happen and don't force it, I'll get it back to even par or under par. You have to be patient, keep on programming positive images, and the results will come eventually.

In contrast to Jack's "Be patient" philosophy, you get a lot of guys who do nothing else but talk about the bad breaks they get. That's a very bad attitude to have. Before you know it, if you keep on visualizing your ball going into trouble, it's going to go into the trouble because the trouble has become your target.

Actually, there is no such thing as luck, really, just a reality. I remember having a big argument with Gibby Gilbert and Grier Jones about it. They were saying, "What do you mean, there's no such things as good breaks, bad breaks, good luck or bad luck?" And

I replied, "If I play twenty years on the tour, I'm not going to get any more good breaks than you. If your ball is landing on the edge of the green all the time, then you're going to bounce into a lot of bunkers, but if you land the ball right in the heart, you're not going to bounce into too many bunkers."

It's my opinion that a lot of people take the bounce out of context. If you're complaining about bouncing into bunkers, it's because you're hitting a bunch of mediocre shots. My theory is that if you hit marginal shots you get marginal breaks. It's the same thing off the tee. If you land the ball on the edge of the fairway with your driver all day, you're going to bounce into a lot of rough, right? When this happens to you, don't make the mistake of saying, "Oh, I got a bad break." That's a bad way of thinking, bad programming.

As I pointed out earlier, before you know it you'll start making the trouble your target instead of just thinking of hitting it to position A on the fairway or to your desired target on the green. The results of such visual images are all too predictable. But there's another thing. Thinking about bad breaks you've had puts your mind in the past and distracts it from what it should be thinking about—hitting the next shot just as well as you can. Too many people carry the last shot with them. It's a heavy and useless burden.

Instead of thinking about bad luck or bad breaks, I think you're better off having the attitude that maybe we do have the ability to will the ball into the hole and that we do have the ability to play super golf, better golf than we've dreamed of. I've seen too many things happen in sports just because a guy wills it to believe otherwise.

It's like that incident I described earlier in the book about Bobby Nichols at the Dow Jones. On the last green he has this enormous putt to make. He hits the putt and there is no way in the world that putt can go in the hole. It's short all the way, but it went in because Bobby "saw" it go in before he ever stroked it.

VISUALIZATION AND YOUR GOALS

The way to evolve as a golfer is always to believe in yourself and believe you are improving and try to improve. You've always got to project to yourself a positive image of your game.

I hear these old guys on the tour, and they say, "Boy, when I was younger, I used to hit the ball so much farther and my irons were fantastic." Well, if I ever get to the point where I am talking about the "old days," you're not going to see me out there on the tour.

Maybe I'll eat those words one day, but, seriously, I tell myself that I hit the ball longer now than I ever did whether I do or not. And Gary Player, who has to be one of the top two players in the world, does the same thing. You will never hear Gary saying that he hit the ball better two weeks ago or two months ago. He always says, "Man, I'm really hitting it now. I've really got it now." He's always living for today and tomorrow.

I really think this is one of the areas of a winning attitude. Never live in the past. Learn from it, but live for today, and work for tomorrow.

I don't ever want to feel that my progression has stopped, and look back to when I was better. I think that's the first sign of a guy going down the drain. It really is true—dwelling on your past glories won't help you now. They just helped you then.

To keep progressing as a golfer, you definitely have to visualize yourself improving all the time. There are a lot of ups and downs in anyone's progress, but you must keep on visualizing your goal. It's like being in a tunnel—you've got to keep on visualizing the ray of light at the other end.

The way to reach your goal in golf is, first, establish your goal, and then break it down into steps. You've got to visualize all the different steps along the way, and then shoot for the first rung of the ladder. For an amateur golfer, the goal might be first, breaking 100, then 90, and so on. On the tour, it would be first qualifying on Mondays, then making the cut, etc. But whatever your goal, it can and must be broken down into realistic little goals along the way.

The reason for the little goals is that no one can just become the greatest golfer in the world overnight. You've got that maybe as your ultimate goal, but each intermediate goal gives you something to aim for in the immediate future that's reasonably in sight. Otherwise, you're going to become very discouraged. I mean, if you say to yourself, "I want to be a great golfer," then you will see yourself down here and the great golfers way up there and there appears no way you can get up to them. But put all those little steps in between and each step on the ladder becomes something you can realistically see yourself achieving.

These litle goals actually become your "choking point." Until each is achieved you will feel pressure. It's like when I first joined the tour, I set my sights on finishing in the top twenty. Then after I'd done that a few times my goal became to finish in the top five, then the top three. My eventual goal, after all these smaller goals had been accomplished, was to win. I can assure you that before I won, I did a lot of choking. But of course, the more you win the easier it becomes to win. Like Nicklaus, for example, he's won so often that he feels the pressure a lot less than the rest of us. I guess his choking point is the "Grand Slam!"

Now all this, of course, takes self-discipline and that's a hard thing. But here, again, visualizing yourself being able to have what it takes is 90 per cent of the battle. Gary Player is a wonderful example of that. He literally talks himself into being as dedicated as he is. Sometimes you almost get the impression that what he says he does is impossible. He would like you to believe that he exercises eight hours a day and practices ten hours a day, and so on. If he's playing golf as well, there wouldn't be enough hours in the day to do it all. But there's a lot of method in his madness, I think. By setting virtually impossible standards for himself, he makes certain that every minute of the day is productive. Great self-discipline is what he's really trying to teach himself. Aim at the impossible, and you achieve a fantastically high standard. We could all benefit from that technique.

In my own way, my thinking is along the same lines as Gary's. I know that, when I can think positively enough, for example, when I shoot those 62's and 63's, when I think I can do anything, then I *can* do just about anything. Maybe I have the ability in my mind to *make* things happen, to make things go my way. In any event, I have a premonition that in maybe five hundred years if you want to move, say, a lamp from one part of the room to another, all you'll have to do is think of this happening and it will be a fact.

This may sound incredible, but I'm firmly convinced we are presently using only 10 per cent of our brain's capabilities in golf and that the only way we can start using the other 90 per cent is to "see ourselves" playing "Pure Golf."

JOHNNY MILLER

Career Tour Victories

1971	Southern Open
1972	Heritage Classic
1973	U. S. Open Championship
1974	Bing Crosby National Pro-Am
	Phoenix Open
	Tucson Open
	Heritage Classic
	Westchester Classic
	Tournament of Champions
	World Open
	Kaiser International
1975	Phoenix Open
	Tucson Open
	Bob Hope Desert Classic
	Kaiser International
1976	NBC Tucson Open
	Bob Hope Desert Classic

Foreign Victories

1972	Otago Classic (New Zealand)
1973	World Cup, Spain, Individual and Team Championship with Jack Nicklaus
	Lancome Trophy, France
1974	Dunlop Phoenix International, Japan
1975	World Cup, Thailand, Individual and Team Championship with Lou Graham
	Dunlop Phoenix International, Japan
1976	British Open Championship

Some Career Highlights

As an amateur Johnny Miller showed early promise by winning the U. S. Junior Championship in 1964 at age seventeen. He qualified for his first U. S. Open at the Olympic Club at the age of nineteen, and finished eighth . . . As a professional, Miller scored a 63 in the 1972 Bob Hope Desert Classic . . . He also scored a 63 in the last round of the 1973 U. S. Open to capture the Championship . . . In 1974 he added the record for the most money won in one season to his successes, his winnings totaling $353,021 that year . . . He scored a 61 in the second round en route to winning the 1975 Phoenix Open, and another 61 in winning the Tucson Open the following week . . . In the 1975 Masters Miller had closing rounds of 65–66, which included six birdies in a row for an outward nine score of 30, breaking all standing Augusta National records . . . He was a member of the 1975 Ryder Cup Team . . . Johnny Miller became a million-dollar money winner at age twenty-eight in January of 1976. In July 1976 he won the British Open Championship at Royal Birkdale by 6 shots, with a record-breaking final round of 66.

Dale Shankland, born and educated in England, is the son of a famous British teaching professional, Bill Shankland. He was formerly staff instructional editor for *Golf* magazine, where he wrote and edited hundreds of articles and studied and analyzed the swing. He is an excellent player and teacher of golf.

Jim McQueen is a golf professional as well as a well-known illustrator.

The Changing Seas

Spring

Paul Humphrey

W
FRANKLIN WATTS

First published in 2007 by
Franklin Watts

© 2007 Franklin Watts

Franklin Watts
338 Euston Road
London NW1 3BH

Franklin Watts Australia
Level 17/207 Kent Street
Sydney, NSW 2000

A CIP catalogue record for this book is available from the British Library

Dewey classification number: 578.4'3

ISBN: 978 0 7496 7162 4

Planning and production by Discovery Books Limited
Editors: Paul Humphrey, Rebecca Hunter
Designer: Jemima Lumley

Photo credits: CFW Images/Chris Fairclough: 8, 10, 11, 12, 13, 19, 25; CFW
Images/EASI-Images: 16 (Neal Cavalier-Smith), 20 and front cover main
(Ed Parker); Chris Fairclough: 28, 29; FLPA: 15 (Martin B Withers), 22
(Nigel Cattlin); Getty Images: front cover bottom, 6 (David Paterson), 9
(Bob Herger), 17 (Bob Elsdale), 18 (John Francis-Blake), 27 (John Giustina);
Istockphoto.com: back cover (Debi Gardiner), 14 (Rob Friedman), title page
and 21 (Svetlana Prikhodkc), 23 (Jim Jurica), 24 (Gord Horne), 26.

Printed in China

Franklin Watts is a division of Hachette Children's Books,
an Hachette Livre UK company.

Contents

Spring is the season that follows winter.

The weather can still be cold
at the beginning of spring.

Crocuses are the first
garden flowers to
appear in spring.

They are followed
later by daffodils.

In spring, young animals are born ...

... and frogspawn
appears in ponds.

Buds on the trees get fatter.

Soon the leaves
begin to grow.

Birds collect grass and twigs to build a nest.

Soon they are busy
feeding baby birds.

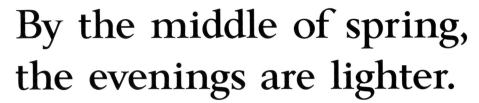

By the middle of spring, the evenings are lighter.

People enjoy
being outside.

Spring weather can be warm and sunny.

But it can be wet and
windy sometimes too!

The trees are full of blossom.

The bees collect
nectar from flowers.

Later in spring, the
frogspawn turns
into tadpoles.

Baby birds are
hungry. Soon they
will learn to fly.

In the farmer's field, the crops are growing.

Sheep enjoy the spring grass.

By the end of spring, the weather is warmer.

We can play outside. Summer is coming!

Spring projects

Collect sticky buds

Buds start to get fatter on the trees in early spring.
By the end of spring, leaves have appeared.

You will need:
A variety of different twig cuttings with buds on
One or two vases of water ✽ Some labels

What to do:

1. Tie a label to each twig cutting with the name of the tree it came from, if you know what it is.

2. Place the different twig cuttings into the vases of water.

3. Watch to see which buds open out into leaves first.

4. Try to identify the trees from their leaves.

Coloured flowers

In the spring, plants need lots of water to help them grow. You can see how this works and make a colourful flower at the same time.

You will need:
A white daisy or carnation
A glass with about 2.5 cm of water ✿ Some food colouring

What to do:

1. Add a tablespoon of food colouring to the water in the glass.

2. Put the flower in the water and leave for 24 hours.

3. The petals of the flower will start to change colour. This is because the flower is taking in the coloured water up its stem.

29

Index